THE
MARKETING
LEADER'S
PLAYBOOK

THE MARKETING LEADER'S PLAYBOOK:

The No Nonsense 7-Step System for
Scaling Your Team and Earning
an Executive Seat

JOSELYNE WALTER

For more information, email information@thediggagency.com

ISBN: 979-8-89694-384-6 - Ebook

ISBN: 979-8-89694-385-3 - Paperback

ISBN: 979-8-89694-386-0 - Hardcover

GET YOUR FREE GIFT!

To get the best experience with this book, I've found that readers who download and use the marketing resources can implement faster and take the next steps needed to scale your team and earn your seat at the table.

You can get a copy by visiting:

https://bit.ly/DiggPlaybook

DEDICATION

To my children (Isaac, Ethan, and Oliver),
who taught me more about prioritization, efficiency,
and meaningful success than any job ever could.

CONTENTS

INTRODUCTION

"So, what do you do for a living?"

It's a simple question, one that is repeatedly asked at networking events, at family gatherings, and when meeting new colleagues. But for me, it was a question I dreaded.

My palms would start sweating, I would feel a nonexistent twitch in one eye, and I would mumble something about being in marketing, then quickly add disclaimers:

"But not the traditional kind!"

"Not like the design-and-colors kind of marketing. Although I wish I had half the talent of creatives."

"Actually… I'm more on the business side of marketing."

Or my favorite disclaimer:

"I actually don't do the logos and pretty stuff."

Why was I so defensive? Because somewhere along the way, marketing got tagged as the "fluff" department. The team that makes pretty things, throws nice events, and picks out color schemes. Or, like a cohort of mine once said during our executive MBA class: *"Marketing is just a picnic every day."*

And sure, some marketers do have what many consider to be "fun" jobs: crafting creative jingles, selecting powerful color schemes, and producing compelling campaigns. And yes, those elements matter. And yes, when the psychology of color is considered, or the visual "feng shui" of angles are accounted for and the craftiness of a message is well selected, it turns out to be powerful marketing. But marketing also has *much more* than that.

Here's what I really wanted to say:

"I've developed pricing strategies that have driven millions in revenue, built marketing departments from scratch and transformed them into growth engines, managed multimillion-dollar budgets, and implemented technology systems that revolutionized how marketing operates."

That's marketing too. The *other* side of marketing.

This book isn't about traditional marketing theory. You won't find the *4 P's* or lengthy discussions about brand psychology here. Instead, this is a practical guide to building and running efficient marketing teams that drive real business results— whether you're a team of one or leading a department of fifty.

I wrote this book because I've been there. I've been the first marketing hire trying to do everything. I've been the director building teams from scratch. I've been the leader transforming traditional marketing departments into modern, efficient operations. And I've learned that success in marketing isn't about having the biggest budget or the largest team. Instead, it's about being resourceful, strategic, and unafraid to try new approaches.

In these pages, you'll discover how to

- build your marketing engine using practical tools and approaches;

- leverage artificial intelligence (AI), freelancers, contractors, and interns effectively;

- create systems that scale as your company scales; and

- navigate career growth in marketing by measuring and communicating your impact in business terms.

I've packed this book with real stories of both successes and failures, as well as actionable tools you can implement immediately. You'll find frameworks for decision-making, templates for common scenarios, and straight talk about what works (and what doesn't).

Whether you're leading a growing team or trying to transform your marketing department, this book is your roadmap to building a marketing operation that delivers real business impact.

HOW TO USE THIS BOOK

Some chapters, especially those covering systems, processes, and operational tactics, are designed to help you *implement* changes in your marketing function and may feel very tactical. Sometimes, they may feel too tactical. I encourage you to bring in your team or manager as you go through these sections. You can assign relevant tasks, share frameworks, and use this book as a discussion tool to guide them in helping you streamline the department.

Marketing isn't a solo sport, and this book is meant to help you maximize your team's impact while maintaining your sanity. And if you are a solo team, then you'll learn how to effectively change this.

Early in the book, I also take a deep dive into artificial intelligence (AI). As Paul Roetzer and Mike Kaput state in the book *Marketing Artificial Intelligence: AI, Marketing, and the Future of Business*, "Your life is already AI-assisted, and your marketing will be, too."[1] AI is growing at such a rapid pace, and the available functionality is only becoming easier to access and implement, so much so that I truly believe it'll revolutionize our way of working in a similar manner that the internet impacted our lives. Therefore, we need to embrace it and learn to allow AI functionality to improve our work

---

[1]   Paul Roetzer and Mike Kaput, *Marketing Artificial Intelligence: AI, Marketing, and the Future of Business* (Dallas, TX: Matt Holt Books, 2022).

processes and styles so that we can more effectively build a scalable marketing team.

I've also included a hefty appendix with more information and references for the frameworks we'll discuss.

Ready to see the other side of marketing? Let's dig in.

FROM TRUCKS TO MARKETING

There were three phones ringing and an alarm going off on my phone for my 10:30 a.m. meeting. It was now 10:45 a.m. I was already late.

The air in the dispatch section felt thick with tension. Computer monitors continuously flickered with new email notification alerts, dispatchers were talking over each other, and a continuous line of customer service reps yelled for attention. Everyone was trying to get an answer to the same urgent question: "Where is my truck?"

A logistics storm was brewing, and I had been thrown straight into its eye.

At the world's largest building product manufacturer, an organization so massive that its 150,000 employees could fill multiple football stadiums, I found myself at the helm of a tiny, overworked dispatch team. Our mission? To move thousands of truckloads of material across North America every month.

Here's what I walked into ...

Julia, my firecracker of a team member, had just been promoted from customer service without a shred of dispatching experience. She was relentless, the kind of person who would push through any challenge. But she also took every comment as a personal attack and had no shortage of complaints of her own.

There was also Gary, who did have dispatching experience, and he was good. Gary was easygoing, well liked, and always talking about his hobbies. But he had a serious time management issue. He was chronically five minutes late. Late for meetings. Late to clock in. Late every single day. But his dispatching was always on time, which was quite a miraculous feat, considering. And he was a wizard with the drivers and the manufacturing plant personnel.

Then, there was my "seasoned" dispatcher: a quiet, steady presence who typed with a single finger while hovering his other hand over the keyboard, creating the illusion of speed. He'd been around long enough to know the ropes and had the attitude of a sweet grandpa who was just happy to be there.

And let's not forget the wildcard, the fourth member of the team, who didn't officially report to me but whose cooperation was essential to our success. She existed in the frustrating gray area of authority, where I needed her to get things done but had no real power over her workload.

This scrappy little team was responsible for moving 36,000 truckloads of building materials across North America every single month. That's right, 36,000!

Some of these orders were leisurely, pre-planned shipments. But many of them were same-day orders, placed in the morning and expected to be on the road by the afternoon. We were juggling a great deal of work, racing against the clock and trying to keep customers happy, all with a team that was, at best, a work in progress.

Here's the kicker: I had zero logistics or dispatching experience myself. But we succeeded. Every day. Every month.

We succeeded by using a variety of strategies:

- Implementing specialized dispatching software connected to our ordering system.

- Leaning heavily on vendor expertise for the software implementation.

- Splitting North America into three regions of the US, plus the Canada region.

- Learning from peers who had previously managed dispatching.

- Moving fast and testing approaches at 40 percent completion, rather than waiting for perfection.

I had to trust the team to handle the daily details, while I coordinated and supported. It was amazing. We also ran into a lot of quirks and kinks. But we learned, we improved, and we got the job done.

Four people. 36,000 truckloads. Every. Single. Month.

I personally had to be very hands-off and trust the team. I was neither the expert nor the one who was going to live with the intricacies and faults of the tool on an hourly basis during work. My role was to coordinate the team, empower them, support them, and push them when needed.

At this time in my career, I was not in marketing. But the lessons I learned in this role stayed with me. They shaped how I see marketing and how I approach every project through a business perspective. Lessons I still employ today.

In early 2014, I found myself in another corporate storm. But this time, it was in a marketing department.

THE MARKETING CHALLENGE

There were eight high-stakes marketing projects on my plate, each one massive, messy, and expected to be completed yesterday. Ten new emails had just come in, all labeled "urgent requests for marketing support" from HR, customer service, and two different plant managers. My unread texts from sales? Thirty-two. My boss? Poking his head in to talk about a "new urgent project." Of course.

The worst part? I wasn't a director. I wasn't an executive. I was just a manager. No budget. No team. No real resources.

Just me, a laptop, and an impossible list of priorities.

I was the sole marketing person at IronHawk Manufacturing, a $500 million international manufacturing company. From day one, I faced what countless marketers would recognize: a to-do list that read like an MBA case study gone rogue.

My projects included the need to rebrand seven acquired companies (each with its own history, identity, and strong opinions on how things *should* be done); merge eight websites into one; field complaints from every business unit about why *their* content was the most important; create new sales materials for varying product lines while developing new templates, establishing clear messaging, and working with a sales team already frustrated by a lack of support; lead and support the implementation of a customer relationship management (CRM) system; support an enterprise resource planning (ERP) system implementation; develop an actual marketing strategy, because there wasn't one, while prioritizing the growth of market share (which first required figuring out what our market share actually *was*); and create a new channel focused on targeting designers and architects.

I was expected to complete all of this with no team to share the workload. There was no budget in place to ease the transition, and I was reporting to a VP of Marketing who changed direction every three hours. This meant that today's top priorities would be tomorrow's abandoned ideas. And a week from then, I'd be asked what my completion date would be for some random idea that would take a heroic effort and that would be forgotten about only until it wasn't.

Sitting in my office that first month, I realized this wasn't just about executing a marketing plan because there was no marketing plan. It felt like stepping onto a massive, ever-shifting chessboard, where the rules changed every few moves. Just as I mapped out a strategy, the board shifted. A competitor launched a new product line, an acquired company's clients voiced concerns, my boss dropped off a new must-do priority project, or regulatory requirements changed overnight.

The clock wasn't just ticking. It was counting down against market opportunities that wouldn't wait, customer relationships that needed immediate attention, and a digital transformation our competitors had started years ago.

But then I remembered my old dispatch team from a few years earlier. The four-person crew that somehow managed 36,000 truckloads of chaos a month. If I could make things work with that team, surely I could figure this out.

This wasn't the kind of chaos that causes panic; instead, it was the kind that every corporate leader knows intimately. The kind that demands equal parts strategy and adaptability.

I attacked marketing the same way I had attacked logistics. I leaned on the expertise of others (agencies and colleagues who were not in marketing); I embraced technology advancements; I onboarded interns and hired freelancers; and I got comfortable with moving fast, which led to failing fast, learning fast, and having a better output.

What started as one person drowning in chaos turned into a structured, high-performing team delivering real business results, all by applying the same principles that had made a tiny dispatch team successful in a giant corporation.

Let me show you how I did it.

For brand work, I hired agencies to help with data collection (brand equity studies, specification share studies, etc.) and customer research.

I then worked with an agency to help vet customer sentiment for our brand, and together we coupled all this data into a recommended brand approach. For this project, I also had to leverage internal colleagues for their support in running the customer surveys, and I even had the help of an IT project manager who had a bit of capacity and was interested in this project.

When it came to the website merger, I brought in an intern who turned out to be fantastic at project coordination, and she was the lead coordinator and liaison between the development/website agency and the internal team.

Sales collateral was a bit different. I worked directly with the sales team to understand what they actually needed (not what we thought they needed). And for help in coordinating it all, I leaned on the same internal IT project manager who had a little capacity and wanted a marketing project to "change things up a little."

And for the large corporate meetings, I leaned on the branding agency and a freelancer to help coordinate these events.

By the end of year one, I had accomplished our goals and had proven enough worth in the "marketing department of one" that I was able to start hiring a team.

By year two, my team had grown to four people, and we brought in a product marketing director.

By year three, our department had doubled in size and increased specification share (a key metric for this company) while maintaining market share and increasing revenue. It felt fulfilling and validating. Can you imagine walking into what felt like a role destined for me to fail in, with no support in terms of people, resources, budget, or mentors, and pushing through to success at this level? Not only did I accomplish our key goals, but I also built a department from scratch and was in this position long enough to see the fruits of our labor. It felt like the sunshine had come out from behind the clouds on a chilly day and instantly warmed me up. I felt proud, accomplished, and good.

Nowadays, I continue to deliver and execute high-impact marketing projects, and I still approach marketing from a business perspective with a focus on *measuring what matters to the business.*

MEASURING WHAT MATTERS TO THE BUSINESS

During any interaction with the C-suite, my peers, or other managers, I would talk about relevant business metrics and show how an investment in marketing would help increase future market share and revenue (something that would impact today's share price). This coupled with the potential of using a CAPEX (capital expenditure) on some projects helped us get a small budget and move faster.

Utilizing CAPEX funds is another corporate trick you can lean on. These funds are set to support specific priority projects and can be used to scale internal resources by hiring a contractor to specifically help deliver said project.

In hindsight, it's easy to outline the work we did and how we did it. But at that time, I was slightly panicking.

Everything seemed urgent. Everything seemed important. But we couldn't do it all at once, and trying to would have meant doing everything poorly. Especially with no resources assigned to me!

The journey from logistics to marketing helped me build a crucial foundation for my marketing approach. This foundation includes applying the same principles of efficiency, prioritization, and resourcefulness to a new challenge.

Whether dispatching 36,000 truckloads a month or leading a one-person marketing team for a $500 million company, success came from using what was available, moving fast, and focusing on impact.

But that poses a new question: What happens when there's simply too much to do and not enough resources to go around? This is something we'll cover in the next chapter.

KEY TAKEAWAYS

Whether managing a logistics team or leading a marketing department, I've learned that in a world of limited resources, trying to do everything means doing nothing well. I also discovered that building a scalable team is actually about implementing the right foundational strategies first.

Before you can build a high-performing marketing engine, scale your operations, or earn your executive seat, you must first master the art of prioritization. Success starts with the ability to look at a mountain of tasks and know exactly where to start digging.

And that's exactly what we'll explore next—how to turn the overwhelming into the manageable, one strategic decision at a time.

HOW DO YOU EAT AN ELEPHANT?

The air buzzes with activity as ten marketing specialists collaborate on upcoming campaigns.

A data analyst is deep-diving into last quarter's metrics on three massive screens, while the social media team huddles around a content calendar in their dedicated creative space. The marketing ops manager just approved a $30,000 testing budget without breaking a sweat. In this company, the marketing department has a $17 million annual budget. Despite this, as a director, you still feel overwhelmed with a long list of projects. Even with all these resources, you still are not able to execute on everything.

Now, let's shift the scene. You're sitting at your desk and running marketing for a manufacturing company. Oh, and the desk is in the middle of a hallway, because there was no more room for another desk. The product catalog, showing the products you are in charge of marketing, is from 1995 and it sits on your shelf because that's what the sales team is still using. You just finished updating the website, which you taught yourself how to do, and now you're racing to prepare a quarterly marketing report. The CEO wants to know why we're not "doing more with social media," and three different sales managers are waiting for you to review their urgent presentation decks. Again, too many projects. Not enough resources.

I've lived both these realities and every shade of gray in between. I've been a director in the sophisticated marketing machine, and I've been that lone marketer trying to modernize a company's entire marketing approach single-handedly.

Yet regardless of whether I was working with a team of thirty or going it alone, one challenge remained stubbornly consistent: There were always too many projects for the team to handle. It was a never-ending flood of projects. And I bet you are in the same situation now. Too many projects. Not enough resources. You need to scale.

But before you can even begin working toward building a scalable team, you must learn to prioritize. In other words, you must determine what work will get done and, more importantly, what work will *not* get done. This is the prerequisite to the seven step system for scaling your team and earning an executive seat. If you do not get this part right, you will inevitably fail. Because doing everything is not possible, nor is it strategic.

DETERMINING THE FIRST BITE

When I was a marketing manager at IronHawk Manufacturing, I had no formal budget and a never-ending list of projects. Everything felt urgent. Everything felt important. And before I even started, I was already behind, with no budget and no resources. I also knew that if I tried to do it all, I'd fail at all of it.

Based on my years of experience outside of marketing, and by sheer definition, I knew that it was impossible for everything to be a top priority. Think about it: It is not possible for multiple items to be number one on a list.

To worsen the situation, the marketing "team" of one was new. As a new department, it was clear that marketing had to prove its worth. Leadership wasn't asking, "How can we invest more in marketing?" They were asking, "Can we even afford it?"

The only way to shift that narrative was to deliver real, measurable impact. And the only way to do *that* was to focus on projects that actually mattered to the business.

Not everything on your to-do list is mission-critical. Not everything deserves your time. If you want to build credibility and scale, you need to ruthlessly prioritize. And prioritization starts by understanding what the business is trying to achieve, then aligning your work with that.

Having an intricate understanding of the business's objectives and goals will help you better determine what projects are aligned with the business and need to be worked on first.

To do this properly, you need to first understand what the business's goals are for the current year and for the next three years. Then align your work and projects with the big-picture objectives of the business. These projects should be at the top of your priority list, and you should have a maximum of five. This is your new priority list, your top five. The ones that will help move the business forward in the right direction.

Now, I know this may sound obvious, but too often, we find ourselves drowning in projects and tasks, and we *think* everything is critical, so we get overwhelmed and reach the verge of burnout. But I can almost guarantee that if you list out every project and critically analyze each one, you will see that a few of those projects will fall toward the bottom of the priority list because they are not directly aligned with the business goals and objectives.

Here is where the challenge comes in: having to say no and deprioritize projects.

Do not overthink this step. Simply list all your projects and tasks, the first twenty-five to thirty projects that come to your mind. List them in a Word document, in Excel, on a napkin, wherever. Do not spend more than ten minutes on this task.

Then, put a star next to the ones that are truly aligned with the business goals and objectives. Here is where you need to be honest and ruthless. Do not look at this from a marketing perspective (as in "We *should* focus on project XYZ"); instead, focus on ruthlessly answering this question: *Does this directly relate to and help us accomplish this year's business goals?* If it doesn't, drop it to the bottom of the list.

Now, this doesn't mean you'll never work on the stuff at the bottom of the list, but you should not invest precious time on the things that your leadership team will not care about. If it doesn't move the business forward, then it should *not* be a top priority.

At the end of this exercise, you should be left with only five projects that you have circled or put a star next to. This is your top five.

Work only on these projects first. Once these are completed, you can then work on the next ones. Remember, not every project can be a top priority, and trying to tackle everything at once is a path to burnout or mediocre work.

This principle of narrowing down to the top five projects stems from a few frameworks. The first is the Pareto Principle, also known as the 80/20 rule, which is the theory that 80 percent of your results come from 20 percent of your efforts. This means your top five projects are likely to deliver most of your results. The second framework is from *Essentialism* by Greg McKeown: "Do less, but better."[2] This is about focusing on what is truly important and having the courage to say no to things that do not align with your highest priorities.

At IronHawk Manufacturing, once I had a vetted list of the projects that were truly priorities, I still needed a framework to determine what incoming projects or requests would become part of the top five as I got through existing projects.

The answer? I used a mix of two frameworks.

The first approach I used was a simple and straightforward question: *What's going to break first if we don't fix it?*

By focusing on the most pressing issues, the ones with immediate business impact, I was able to focus on quick wins, build credibility, and demonstrate marketing's role as a driver of growth rather than just a cost center. This approach, combined with tracking and communicating the right business-driven tasks, is what ultimately led to real investment in marketing.

The other framework I constantly relied on was the Impact/Effort framework.

---

[2]   Greg McKeown, *Essentialism: The Disciplined Pursuit of Less* (New York: Crown Currency, 2014).

We'll cover both prioritization frameworks in the next section. Proving marketing's worth is also an entire conversation on its own, one we will cover in Step 5: Proving Your Worth.

PRIORITIZATION FRAMEWORKS

As I mentioned, the way I navigated through my long list of urgent requests was by asking myself, "What's going to break first if we do *not* fix it?" This is the Impact vs. Explosion assessment. It's a ruthless prioritization framework used to ensure we focus on what truly matters. At its core, the Impact vs. Explosion framework is a decision-making tool designed to help determine which projects will drive meaningful results and which ones, if ignored, will lead to serious consequences.

In dispatch, it was simple. If trucks don't move, nothing else matters. In marketing, it's trickier, but the principle is the same. You need to know what's critical, what can wait, and what's just nice to have.

To apply this framework, I started by defining impact, asking myself what would happen if we executed a project successfully. I considered whether it would improve efficiency or create long-term value. Then I defined the explosion factor by asking what would break if we did nothing at all. Would the business lose money? Would it cause operational chaos? Would it damage the company's reputation? Would my job be at risk?

What became clear was that just because something had a high impact did not mean it was urgent. Some projects had significant upsides and would provide long-term value, but they could be delayed without immediate consequences. Others, which seemed less critical on the surface, could create major disruptions if left unaddressed.

This framework forced me to think differently about prioritization. Instead of reacting to every request as if it were a top priority, I began making strategic decisions about where to invest time and resources. Some projects needed immediate attention, while others could be phased out over time or pushed to a later date without negative consequences—even if that made me feel extremely uncomfortable. This approach also made it easier to avoid the trap of responding to the loudest internal stakeholders rather than focusing on what actually moved the business forward.

This process involves a mindset shift. You need to start asking what would happen if something does not get done. Will clients and customers take their business away from you? Will you have a public relations crisis? Will your revenue or profitability be negatively impacted? With this clarity, I applied the framework to my workload and quickly saw the results.

Here's how it works:

Impact: What will happen if we do this well?

Explosion: What will break if we don't do this at all?

To give an example, let's consider those disparate websites that came under my ownership after multiple acquisitions. We had seven different websites that needed to be merged, and each one was carrying its own branding, content, and internal politics. It was a mess.

The *impact* of merging them would be a better user experience, a consistent brand, and easier maintenance for our internal team. The *explosion* if we didn't merge them would be inefficient operations but overall minimal impact to customers because there would be no change to their day-to-day operations and methods of ordering. Nothing would break. It was important, but not urgent. So immediately, I knew this did not meet the explosion litmus test and could therefore be deprioritized.

I then applied this framework to updating sales materials. The impact of updating the collateral would be a polished, professional presentation that would build credibility. The explosion would be the sales team creating their own materials with various font types and sizes and copyright-infringing Google images. At worst—and this did happen—the sales team would also create new features and product promises that were technically wrong and posed a legal risk! The sales materials couldn't wait. We were losing sales because we didn't have the right tools to communicate our product offerings and our sales team was having a hard time converting sales. Clearly, the sales materials had greater explosion risks and had to be prioritized over the website work.

As I thought about it, I was convinced that the websites could wait a few months. The planning and content creation alone would take months to develop anyway, and the end user and our key stakeholders would not see the benefit of this work until at least nine months down the road. This led me to the uncomfortable decision that we could start the internal content work slowly, mapping out the timeline to minimize the expense, while focusing on the immediate wins of sales materials.

Also, delivering quick wins (sales getting their new materials) helped us build credibility. It helped bridge relationships (sales were happy with us), it helped them increase their sales, and it helped our marketing ROI metrics. The alternative was to work on the website and have nothing to show for months, even a year. Can you imagine that? A year with no improvements or deliverables?

While lowering the priority of overhauling our websites might seem controversial to many of my fellow marketers, the truth is, we still made progress toward it. The brand work would be the foundation needed to build the appropriate messaging, look, and feel for the website. Furthermore, this lowering of prioritization allowed us to prioritize another big initiative (samples program), which was critical to our specification share and making sales.

This isn't some complex scoring system. It's about asking practical questions that force clarity and cut through the noise. When everything feels important—and as a marketer, you are likely clouded with thoughts like "We *should* be doing XYZ"—these questions can help separate the urgent matters from the distractions and the essentials from the nice-to-haves.

Here are a few other thought-provoking questions to ask when applying the Impact vs. Explosion assessment.

The first question is *"What's actually breaking right now?"* This isn't about what is inefficient, outdated, or could be improved. It's about identifying what is actively causing pain at this moment. By asking this question first, you can start navigating to what should be the top priorities.

The second question is *"What can we fix quickly with our current resources?"* Not every issue requires a major overhaul, a new budget, or months of planning. Some problems can be resolved with a strategic shift, a small process change, or a quick-win solution. This question forces prioritization based not just on need but on feasibility. It helps avoid the trap of focusing solely on large, long-term projects while immediate problems remain unsolved.

If something can be addressed within days or weeks with the people, tools, and budget already available, it should be considered as part of your top five for immediate attention. These quick fixes don't just solve problems; they also build momentum and credibility for the marketing function and key stakeholders. This goes back to showing results fast. As you probably know, especially if you're in the corporate space, it's all about "What have you done for me lately?" Showing continuous results and wins is critical.

The final question is *"What needs a longer-term solution?"* Some problems are too big for a quick fix. They require deeper investment, broader buy-in, or systemic change. This question helps separate what must be planned out for the long run rather than reacted to in the moment.

If a major issue can't be solved now, the next step is to build a roadmap. Who needs to be involved? What dependencies exist? How will this be executed over time without disrupting other priorities? Thinking long-term allows for smart allocation of time and resources rather than constantly reacting to what feels urgent today at the expense of what will truly drive impact in the future.

These questions may seem simple, but they are powerful because they create discipline. They force you to move beyond gut reactions and dig into what is truly urgent, actionable, and strategic. They also provide clarity when dealing with competing priorities and stakeholders, ensuring that the agenda isn't being set by the loudest voice in the room but by the business realities of what must be addressed first.

So far, we've used two approaches to reduce a long list of projects down to a manageable top five. Dare I say, we now have an approach for how to start "eating the elephant!"

If you still have more than five top projects, you can use the Impact/Effort Matrix to help you narrow down the list. Like the Impact vs. Explosion method, this one is not fancy. You simply take all your projects and plot them based on two concepts: (1) how much impact the project will have on the business, and (2) how much effort or resources it will take to complete. The sweet spot? High-impact, low-effort projects.

These are your quick wins, the ones that move the business forward and build credibility fast. On the other end, you'll spot the high-effort, low-impact projects. These are the ones that suck up time, drain your team, and don't drive real results. They need to be either deprioritized, delegated, or killed altogether. Using this matrix will help you take emotion out of the decision-making process. It will force you to ask the hard questions: Is this project worth it? Will leadership care about this outcome? Will it move the business forward? And most importantly, do I have the resources to get it done *well*?

The impact/effort matrix
A simple approach to prioritizing work.

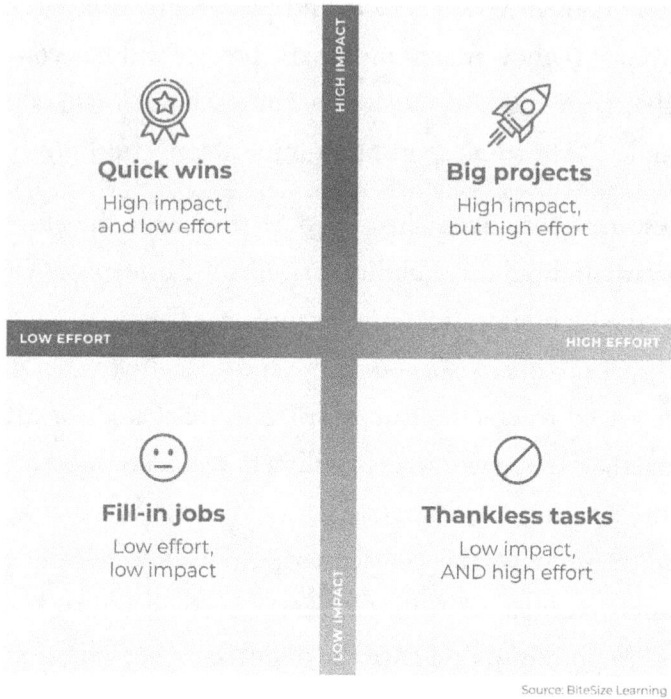

Quick wins
High impact,
and low effort

Big projects
High impact,
but high effort

Fill-in jobs
Low effort,
low impact

Thankless tasks
Low impact,
AND high effort

HIGH IMPACT

LOW EFFORT

HIGH EFFORT

LOW IMPACT

Source: BiteSize Learning

When I applied this approach to my workload, the results were immediate. I could finally separate what needed my attention now, what could be handled with a few adjustments, and what required a structured long-term plan. It also gave me the confidence to professionally articulate what the marketing priorities were and why: my top five.

At IronHawk Manufacturing, this led us to the following outcomes:

1. Fixing sales materials first (quick win, prevent immediate damage). This priority also gave us the following wins:

   - Leveraging sales as a resource (they immediately became huge fans and supporters of our work, many of them serving as an extension of our team for some projects)

   - Showing, based on qualitative and quantitative feedback, how the marketing collateral helped sales reduce their sales closing cycle

   - Showing measurable impact to our revenue due to a marketing investment (thus allowing us to ask for the budget to help build a new website)

2. Starting website planning (long-term project, needed proper planning)

3. Conducting customer and brand equity research

4. Beginning brand consolidation (gradual process done in phases)

5. Investing time and resources in overhauling our samples program

This prioritization also gave us room to allow for other high-impact projects that helped cut costs and improve profitability.

Prioritizing work using these frameworks and focusing on narrowing the work down to the top five projects allowed me to put a realistic lens on the timing to deliver each goal and show impactful wins. It also yielded an effective year in which we hit our goals!

"SQUEAKY WHEEL" SYNDROME AND HOW TO OVERCOME IT

In many organizations, marketing teams often fall victim to "squeaky wheel" syndrome—that is, a situation where the loudest, most persistent voices get priority, rather than the most strategic or impactful initiatives. This can come from sales teams demanding last-minute pitch decks, executives pushing pet projects, or internal stakeholders flooding marketing with urgent (but low-value) requests. When marketing operates in reactive mode, constantly addressing whoever yells the loudest, strategy takes a back seat, and this can lead to burnout, inefficiency, and missed growth opportunities.

Examples of Squeaky Wheel Syndrome in Marketing:

1. **Sales fire drills**

    A sales rep insists they need a custom one-off presentation ASAP to land a big client. Marketing drops everything to create it—only to find out later the deal was never that serious. Meanwhile, a high-impact demand generation campaign gets delayed.

2. **The CEO's latest idea**

    An executive reads an article on a new trend—AI, NFTs, experiential marketing—and suddenly, marketing is expected to shift gears and launch an initiative around it. No data supports its relevance, but leadership pressure forces the team to redirect resources.

3. **Endless internal requests**

HR wants a recruitment video, Customer Service wants an FAQ sheet, IT wants a branded internal dashboard. None of these requests drive core business goals, but because these teams are persistent, marketing spends valuable time fulfilling them.

The real danger of squeaky wheel syndrome is that it creates a cycle where marketing is constantly chasing tasks instead of driving impactful projects and initiatives. When marketing teams become order-takers, they lose control of their time, their impact, and ultimately, their credibility. Each of these examples illustrates how reactive work can quietly drain resources.

In order to overcome squeaky wheel syndrome, you need to use a proven prioritization framework so that the decisions on what to work on don't become an emotional debate.

You can use the two frameworks covered in this chapter: Impact vs. Explosion and the Impact/Effort framework.

You can also use the Eisenhower Matrix (shown below) to evaluate incoming requests (a summarized overview of all these frameworks are in Appendix A).

Add ROI and long-term impact to help you "break a tie" between initiatives. If a request doesn't align with the business's core goals, it should get deprioritized or denied.

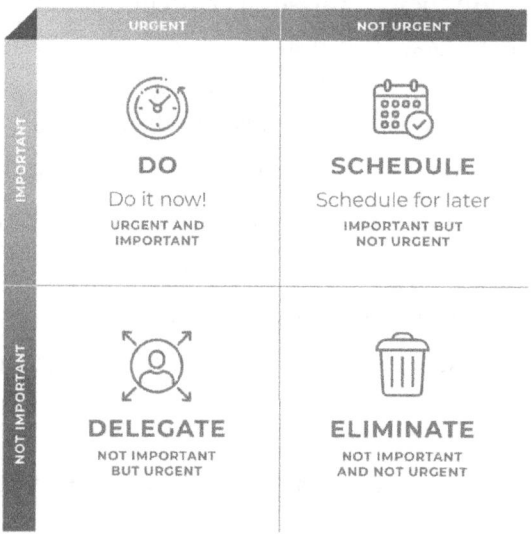

Other ways you can limit squeaky wheel syndrome include the following:

- **Create a marketing request process**

  Implement a structured intake process where all requests must be submitted through a form that includes business justification, expected outcomes, deadlines, and the basics of a creative brief. This forces stakeholders to think critically before making demands.

- **Align with leadership on strategic priorities**

  Set clear, data-driven marketing goals that leadership agrees on at the start of the quarter or year. Then, when the next "urgent" request comes in, you can point back to agreed-upon priorities and ask, "Where does this fit in?"

- **Say no (or "not now") with data**

  Pushback is easier when supported by numbers. If an idea doesn't align with revenue goals, market trends, or customer needs, show the data. Instead of simply declining, offer an alternative: "Based on our priorities, we're focusing on X. Let's revisit this in Q3 when we review initiatives."

- **Be intentional with you time**

  Let's break this down into more detail.

It's easy for marketing leaders to get trapped in the daily grind: endless meetings, urgent requests, and reactive work that keeps the business running but doesn't push it forward. To break out of this cycle, you need to intentionally carve out time to focus on long-term, strategic initiatives that drive business growth and sustainability. Being intentional will help you better overcome squeaky wheel syndrome because you'll have a clear vision of the future of the business and the types of projects that will push the business forward.

A good rule of thumb? Spend at least 70 percent of your time working *on* the business (big-picture initiatives) and only 30 percent working *in* the business (day-to-day execution). For mid-sized businesses or those in a transition, the split may be closer to 60 percent on and 40 percent in. The point is to lean more toward working *on* the business.

To do this effectively, you need to

- **Understand the business's goals (one to three years).** What are the company's long-term goals? Where does leadership see the organization heading? Marketing should be proactively supporting these objectives, not just reacting to short-term needs.

- **Know what's important to your stakeholders.** Your executive team and board members have priorities that impact decision-making. If marketing aligns with these, it becomes a revenue driver, not just a cost center.

- **Lead strategic projects that impact long-term growth.** Whether it's brand positioning, digital transformation, customer experience improvements, or market expansion, marketing should be spearheading initiatives that shape the company's future, not just executing on requests.

Protecting time for big-picture thinking ensures marketing isn't just keeping up but also leading the way. You will help redefine marketing's role in the business and position yourself as a strategic partner in growth.

Overall, the loudest voices (squeaky wheel) shouldn't dictate marketing's roadmap. Without clear guardrails, the squeaky wheel drains time, stifles strategy, and reduces marketing to an internal task rabbit.

But by setting clear priorities, creating structured intake processes, aligning with leadership, saying no, and being intentional with your time, marketing can stay in control. And if all else fails? Push the request back with one simple question: "What's the budget for this?" If they want it badly enough, they'll fund it. And if not? They'll stop asking. Either way, marketing wins.

KEY TAKEAWAYS

Whether you're a solo marketer or leading a team of thirty, the challenges remain the same: too many projects, too few resources, and constant pressure from competing priorities.

So the next time you are overwhelmed, try not to "oil the squeaky wheel" or tackle what you *think* marketing should be working on. Instead, outline your project list by first aligning each project with the business's goals and objectives. Narrow down this list to only the top five projects.

Once you've narrowed down to a list of business-impactful projects, you can then use the Impact vs. Explosion framework to start prioritizing within these projects. Remember, the Impact vs. Explosion framework provides a practical way to cut through the noise and focus first on what truly matters. For each initiative, ask the following practical questions: (1) What's actually breaking right now? (2) What can we fix quickly with our current resources? (3) What needs a longer-term solution?

As you are left with a smaller (yet likely still long) list of projects, you can apply the Impact/Effort framework to determine which projects you should work on first. This framework will allow you to plot all projects against each other in a visual way. You can also utilize the Eisenhower Matrix to help you determine what projects are worth investing your limited time in.

Remember, you have permission to ruthlessly prioritize. Being ruthless is about making sure what you do actually matters. It's about feeling more in control, less overwhelmed, and confident that you're working on the right things. And yes, some of these decisions will make you uncomfortable.

As we move into the next chapter, we'll explore how to build and scale your marketing engine. Because knowing what to do first is only half the battle. The other half is building a system that can deliver consistently and grow with your business.

FIX THE LEAKS FIRST

Are you too busy paddling to notice your boat is filling with water? Talk about being inefficient!

Think of inefficiencies like holes in a bucket. When water levels drop, the instinct is to pour more water in. In the case of marketing, that's more resources, more budget, more people. It seems like the obvious fix, but if the bucket is full of leaks, you're just wasting effort and money. The real solution? Fix the leaks first.

It sounds simple, yet you'd be surprised how many companies keep pouring instead of patching.

"Every project, if we can even find it in our system, is past due. My emails are all filled with angry notes from requestors reminding me how we've disappointed them. My team hasn't had a win in months," Simon said, sounding defeated.

It was true: For this team, deadlines were slipping, morale was tanking, and everyone insisted we needed to hire another designer. As the marketing director, my job was to just fix it! And both my boss and Simon, my peer, thought the fix was to hire another designer. But my gut told me this was not a headcount issue.

So, I pushed against their hard recommendation of approving a new hire and instead spent a couple of weeks observing the team. As I analyzed their workflow data, a different story emerged. I noticed designers frequently asking the same kinds of questions:

"Has anyone seen the logo from the Johnson campaign?"

"Does anyone have the original files from last year's holiday campaign?"

I tracked their time logs and saw countless hours vanishing into these searches. In project retrospectives, I uncovered a pattern of last-minute requests from other departments, pushing planned work aside. The data was revealing: Marketing would request rush campaigns that could have been scheduled weeks earlier, and sales needed "emergency" presentations that were actually for meetings set months ago. Looking deeper into their project archives, I found multiple versions of similar designs scattered across different team drives, as well as completed projects that never made it past the first client meeting. The real problems were hiding in plain sight, and they were *not* in the team's size; they were in the team's systems and processes.

- **15 percent** of their time was spent searching for existing assets.

- **30 percent** of projects were rush jobs that could have been planned.

- **20 percent** of designs were never used.

- **15 percent** of the work was duplicated across teams.

Hiring another designer would have helped in the short term but ignored the deeper issues causing inefficiency. Instead, we fixed the leaks:

1. **We organized their digital asset management system** to make finding assets easier. This was completed by implementing a more efficient filing system and folder naming convention.

2. **We streamlined the project intake process** to prioritize and plan work better. We implemented a project intake questionnaire that gave us more detail up front and also set the expectations for turnaround time.

3. **We built a shared project calendar** to reduce duplication and last-minute rushes.

4. **We developed a service level agreement** to set expectations for the team's turnaround time and also ensure our internal team was aware of the turnaround time expected from them.

The result? A 30 percent increase in team capacity—without adding headcount. Better yet, the team felt less stressed, became more productive, and had the time to focus on quality work.

The lesson from the creative team was clear: The issue wasn't a lack of people, but a lack of structure. Their bucket had leaks. Fixing these inefficiencies gave them capacity they didn't even realize they had.

This experience and other similar ones solidified a lesson I've carried ever since: When faced with resource constraints, try to resist the temptation of adding more water (in the form of people or tools) to your bucket that likely has holes. Instead, start by asking what you can fix.

In order to effectively do this, you need to mentally remove the option of adding resources (people or tools) to fix the problem.

Look for the root cause using the 5 Whys method. The 5 Whys is a problem-solving technique that helps identify the root cause of a problem by repeatedly asking "Why?" until the true underlying issue is uncovered. Once you identify the true root cause of the problem, you can solve the issue.

Too often, teams focus on surface-level symptoms rather than addressing the real cause of inefficiencies. Or worse, they hire additional people or invest in expensive tools only to find that the same problem persists. The 5 Whys method forces deeper thinking by tracing a problem back to its origin, ensuring that solutions are addressing the actual issue rather than just putting a temporary fix in place.

Let's dig into the 5 Whys.

I learned this technique early in my career, when I was working with the world's largest manufacturer, Exto Manufacturing. This company was big on lean manufacturing and had adopted the Kaizen approach.

Kaizen (Japanese for "improvement") is a concept that impacts all business activities and focuses on continuously improving all functions. It involves all employees, from the CEO to the frontline workers. The goal of Kaizen is to create a culture of continuous improvement, aiming toward small incremental improvements of 1 percent every day.

The gist is that you document a process, review the current state, and develop a plan for improvement. The goal isn't to get to the perfect solution; the goal is to improve from the current state. Remember, it's about small incremental improvements. Then you measure and do it again. Review and fix what doesn't work. It's a state of continuous improvement.

Kaizen is a phenomenal concept that has been ingrained in me ever since I learned it. The technique has even trickled through to my personal life. If we aim for a small 1 percent change every day, can you imagine how different our lives can look in thirty, sixty, and even ninety days?!

While Kaizen is often used in operations and manufacturing, it's just as effective in marketing when applied to resource challenges. Note that I won't walk you through all the details of Kaizen and how to implement it, although I will include a few resources in the appendix.

To get you started with this approach, I challenge you to start thinking about the "why" behind the process that is causing a problem. First, start with determining the problem statement. What is the problem you are seeing or trying to solve? Then ask, "Why?" This may help you uncover fundamental issues causing inefficiency, waste, or bottlenecks. Then start the process again, asking the same question: "Why?" Do this five times.

By doing this enough, you'll often find that you do not need additional headcount or a fancy, expensive tool. Instead, you can probably gain efficiency and more capacity by streamlining a process or eliminating unnecessary steps. If your team is new and you don't have a formal process for certain tasks yet, this is a good time to build them.

Here's how to use this step-by-step approach, illustrated with a detailed marketing example:

STEP 1: START WITH THE PROBLEM STATEMENT

Clearly define the issue at hand. For example:

"The marketing team is constantly missing campaign deadlines."

STEP 2: ASK "WHY?" UNTIL YOU REACH THE ROOT CAUSE

Each "Why" leads to the next layer of insight. Here's how it might play out:

1. **"Why are we missing deadlines?"**

    Because tasks take longer than expected to complete.

2. **"Why do tasks take longer than expected?"**

    Because there are too many revisions and feedback loops.

3. **"Why are there so many revisions?"**

    Because the creative team doesn't fully understand the campaign goals at the start.

4. **"Why doesn't the creative team understand the goals?"**

    Because there's no clear brief provided at the project kickoff.

5. **"Why isn't there a clear brief?"**

    Because we don't have a standardized briefing process.

STEP 3: ADDRESS THE ROOT CAUSE

The root cause in this case is the **lack of a standardized briefing process.** Simply adding more designers or extending deadlines wouldn't solve the underlying issue. Instead, you could try the following solutions:

- Create a clear and repeatable briefing template.

- Train stakeholders on how to complete the brief before submitting requests.

- Assign a project manager to ensure briefs are complete before kickoff.

The result? Fewer revisions, better collaboration, and on-time delivery. All without adding resources.

A critical tip for using the 5 Whys approach is to stay focused on facts, not assumptions. This can be done by using data or real examples to support your answers as you work through the questioning. Trust me, this is not as obvious as you think. Consider how often someone answers a question with the words "I feel …" or "I think it's because …" rather than pointing to specific evidence.

When using the 5 Whys, speculation and opinions can lead you down the wrong path, resulting in misdiagnosed problems and ineffective solutions. Instead, every response should be backed by real data, concrete observations, or firsthand experience. For example, "Why aren't sales teams using the marketing collateral?" "All marketing collateral is readily available in our digital asset management (DAM) system, but data shows that the sales team is not downloading the documents." The direct feedback from sales is that the collateral does not meet their needs. "Why doesn't it meet their needs?" And on and on.

Another important factor in successfully using the 5 Whys is involving the right people in the process, especially those closest to the problem. These "frontline" workers often have the most insight.

If designers are struggling with constant revisions, it's not enough to ask their managers why; you need to speak directly to the designers themselves. They are the ones navigating the day-to-day challenges, and they will have the best insights into the inefficiencies creating delays—and likely the causes behind them.

Finally, avoid finger-pointing by engaging in honest and open dialogue. This method isn't about placing blame on individuals but rather uncovering systemic issues that might be causing inefficiencies. It's easy for teams to become defensive when discussing what's not working, but shifting the mindset to problem-solving rather than finger-pointing leads to better outcomes.

If a team discovers that a major roadblock exists because one department failed to communicate properly, the takeaway shouldn't be about blaming that department but about identifying how to improve communication going forward.

This is very difficult to do, so I find that the most effective solution is to give everyone the benefit of the doubt. By immediately assuming the best intentions in others, you will prevent yourself from coming across as judgmental. For example, if one department didn't communicate properly, thinking of reasons why this might have happened will put you into problem-solving mode. Did the communication not go through because they were waiting for some final feedback before sending approvals? Did they communicate to the wrong person without realizing the leadership team or the designers needed to get involved?

APPLYING THE 5 WHYS TO MARKETING COLLATERAL NOT BEING USED

To see how this works in action, let's look at a common issue: Marketing teams spend countless hours creating sales collateral, but then the sales team doesn't use it. Instead of assuming the collateral is simply ineffective, we can apply the 5 Whys to dig deeper into the root cause.

The first question we ask is "Why aren't sales teams using the marketing collateral?" The immediate response is that they say it doesn't meet their needs. That leads us to the next question: "Why doesn't it meet their needs?" The answer could be that the materials fail to address the specific questions their customers ask during the sales process.

Now, we push further: "Why don't the materials address customer questions?" Sadly, it turns out the marketing team wasn't aware of what customers were actually asking the sales team members. So we ask, "Why didn't marketing involve sales in the content creation process?" At this stage, we start uncovering structural inefficiencies. The reason marketing didn't include sales in the process is that there is no formal process in place for collaboration between these teams.

Finally, we ask, "Why isn't there a formal process for sales and marketing collaboration?" The answer: Historically, these teams have worked in silos. There has never been an established way for sales and marketing to align on messaging, customer objections, or the real needs of prospects.

By the time we reach this final "Why," we've moved past the symptom (sales not using marketing materials) and uncovered the root cause: a lack of structured collaboration between sales and marketing. The real solution isn't just reworking the collateral; it's building a formal process for sales and marketing alignment so that future materials are informed by real sales conversations and customer needs. We can even take this a step further and require that designers visit with sales and customers once a quarter so that they can get firsthand experience and knowledge on what customers are looking for and what matters to them.

This is the power of the 5 Whys. Instead of reacting with surface-level fixes, you have a structured way to identify the deeper issues and implement solutions that actually solve the problem at its core.

APPLYING THE 5 WHYS IN RESOURCE DECISIONS

I was having lunch with a marketing leader of a construction company. She was talking to me about how overwhelmed she was with projects and how she was burning out quickly. She had a couple of agencies helping her with very specific tasks, but there were still too many projects on her plate that were all competing for prioritization. She wanted to hire an intern or some support, but she couldn't find enough time to even think about what to outsource!

This is a common problem I've heard from many leaders. During our conversation, I walked her through the 5 Whys to help her get to the root of some of the "problems" she felt she had to solve right away.

The first thing she brought up was the need for a DAM tool. Based on my experience with various marketing departments of varying sizes, I instinctively knew that implementing a DAM was almost certainly not urgent. I ran this "priority project" through my litmus test of Impact vs. Explosion, and sure enough, this project was not a priority.

I then helped her navigate through this issue using the 5 Whys. My friend started with this:

"I need to find a suitable DAM system, within budget, get it approved, and go through the full process of implementing it, including determining the folder structures, filing system, and tags for all files. I don't know how I'm going to get this done!"

I asked her, "Why does your company *need* a DAM?"

She couldn't really answer the question with facts. Her reasoning was mainly rooted in the fact that "all real marketing departments have a DAM."

It turns out, there wasn't a dire need for a DAM. She just felt like this was something she *had* to do as a marketing leader. In reality, their current system for tracking and hosting project images was sufficient for their business. A DAM would've been nice to have, but most certainly wasn't a must-have.

Through additional questioning, we landed on the real problem. It was the fact that the existing assets were poorly organized and tagged, making them hard to find unless you were the project manager who led that project and uploaded the images directly into the shared drive. The conversation went a little like this:

"Why are files hard to find?"

"Because the files are organized by year and not by project type. There is also no logical tagging, so searching for certain terms yields no results."

"Why are assets poorly organized?"

"The files are uploaded to the server by the project managers, whenever they get around to it. So the naming conventions of the files vary depending on which project manager uploaded the files."

"Why hasn't a standardized system been implemented?"

"I don't know. The project manager simply uploads files when they remember to do it."

"Why are teams working in silos?"

"Maybe there has never been formal ownership over asset management, leaving file storage as an afterthought rather than a structured process."

By the time we reached the root cause, it was clear that the problem was not a lack of a DAM tool but the lack of an effective system for organizing and managing assets. Instead of immediately investing in expensive software, the solution was to fix the organizational system first, to outline the process of uploading images with the appropriate tags and naming conventions.

As you continue down this path of continuous improvement, you will inevitably get to a point where you need to invest in a tool so that you can gain more efficiencies or improve a persistent problem. This is a great point to be at! Once you know your process is lean and efficient, then yes, move on to the next step of investing in a tool to continue down the continuous improvement path.

USING THE 5 WHYS FOR RESOURCE DECISIONS

1. Clearly define the problem.

2. Involve key team members for accurate insights.

3. Keep asking "Why?" until you uncover the root cause. The rule of thumb is to ask "Why?" five times.

4. Verify the root cause with data or examples.

5. Develop solutions that address the root cause—not just the symptoms.

Closing Example: A Tale of Two Teams

At BrandForge Studios, a mid-sized agency in Seattle, the content marketing team was falling behind on their client deliverables. Blog posts were late, social media calendars had gaps, and client satisfaction scores were dropping. The CMO, looking at the mounting backlog, made what seemed like an obvious decision: hire two additional writers at $85,000 per year each. Six months and $170,000 later, the same problems persisted. The team was still missing deadlines, and now there was the added complexity of coordinating more writers. Why? Because the real issue was a lack of clarity in content strategy.

Writers were spending hours in meetings debating content direction, creating similar pieces for different clients, and reworking articles multiple times because the initial direction wasn't clear.

Meanwhile, Ignition Brand Co., a direct competitor facing similar challenges, took a different approach. When their campaign launch times stretched from six to twelve weeks, the VP of Marketing was ready to expand the team. But first, they applied the 5 Whys:

Why are campaigns launching late? Because we're waiting on legal approval.

Why is legal approval taking so long? Because we're sending them complete campaigns for review, and by the time campaigns are approved by key stakeholders, we are running late.

Why are we sending complete campaigns? Because that's how we've always done it.

Why haven't we tried sending components earlier? Because we don't have a process for partial reviews.

Why don't we have that process? Because we never identified legal reviews as the bottleneck.

The solution? Restructure the workflow to send key campaign messages and claims to legal while designers were still working on visuals. They created a "legal brief template" that highlighted key claims for quick review, and they scheduled standing weekly meetings with the legal team. The result? Campaign launch times dropped to two weeks, faster than their original timeline, without hiring a single new person.

COMMON PITFALLS TO AVOID

While the 5 Whys method is a powerful tool for uncovering root causes, it is easy to fall into common traps that can limit its effectiveness. One of the biggest mistakes is stopping too soon, usually after the first or second "Why."

When teams settle for surface-level answers, they risk addressing only the symptoms rather than the deeper issue. It is essential to keep asking "Why?" until the fundamental cause is revealed.

Another common pitfall is jumping to solutions too quickly. There is a natural tendency to want to fix problems immediately, but making changes before fully understanding the root cause can lead to ineffective solutions and wasted effort. The goal of the 5 Whys is not to treat symptoms but to ensure that any solution implemented is targeting the real issue at its core.

Finally, it is important to avoid overcomplicating the process. The 5 Whys is a straightforward method for problem-solving, but some teams turn it into a drawn-out, overly complex analysis. The key is to stay focused on clear, fact-based reasoning and not let the process become bogged down by unnecessary details. Keeping it simple, structured, and focused on facts will lead to the best results.

KEY TAKEAWAYS

The 5 Whys is a mindset shift. Instead of dealing with surface-level problems ("We need more people"), it pushes you to uncover root causes ("We need better processes"). In marketing, that's often the difference between a quick fix that drains resources and a smart solution that creates lasting improvement.

Whether your team is overwhelmed, deadlines are slipping, or quality is suffering, resist the temptation to immediately throw more resources at the problem. Instead, take a step back, analyze the situation, and fix the leaks.

Because once you fix the leaks in your bucket, you'll find that your existing team and tools can go much further than you thought possible.

In the next chapter, we'll take this process one step further by exploring technology and tools that can help improve efficiencies. Because while fixing the system is critical, knowing when and where to strategically invest for future growth is equally important. Let's dive in.

TECHNOLOGY AND AI TOOLS THAT ACTUALLY HELP

"Kim, you have sixty days to fix this or we'll need to make changes." The message was clear: fix the chaos or lose her job. The countdown had begun.

This story is about a colleague of mine who taught me how *not* to implement new technology.

Kim was the creative director at Rockwell & Sons Manufacturing, and her department had earned an infamous nickname: "the black hole." It was a serious problem that was affecting the entire business. Marketing campaigns were delayed. Sales teams couldn't get their presentation decks on time. Product launches were held up, waiting for packaging designs. Projects would enter her department and seemingly disappear into a void of uncertainty.

"What's the status of the trade show materials I requested last week?" a sales director would ask.

"Let me check," Kim would respond, frantically digging through emails and folders.

"When will the new product catalog be ready?" the CEO would inquire during leadership meetings.

"We're...working on it," Kim would mumble, feeling her face flush.

The final straw came during a particularly tense executive meeting. The CMO, David, pulled her aside afterward, his expression grim. "Kim, you have sixty days to fix this or we'll need to make changes."

Panic set in. Kim dove into research mode, scheduling demos with every project management vendor she could find. She was moving at a frantic pace, barely sleeping, desperate to find something that could bring order to the chaos. That's when she found what seemed like the perfect solution: a platform that promised to do it all. Project tracking? Check. Asset management? Check. Budget tracking? That was a bonus she hadn't even considered.

Kim invited me to join a vendor call, and I could hear the relief in her voice as she described the tool. "This is it," she said, her words tumbling out rapidly. "This will fix everything. We can track every project, store all our assets, *and* manage our budgets."

The desperation was palpable. The creative tracking piece could indeed be valuable—their current system was essentially a graveyard of outdated spreadsheets and unanswered emails. The budget tracking seemed unnecessary but harmless enough. We were using basic Excel sheets with only two columns, so any improvement would be welcome.

But as we started the implementation, red flags began appearing. The budget feature turned out to be a beta version, and it was barely functional. The asset management system would duplicate our existing DAM, creating more confusion. Worst of all, the workflow would require a complete overhaul of the department's processes—processes that, as we discovered, barely existed in the first place.

Then came the bombshell: Kim was let go before the implementation was complete. I inherited the mess, and what I found was staggering. The project tracker was a manual spreadsheet that often went weeks without updates. Designer workloads were a mystery. No one had defined what constituted a "small" versus a "large" project. There weren't even basic standards for project requests—some came through email, some through hallway conversations, and some were simply assumed.

We spent six painful months trying to build a sophisticated system on a foundation of chaos. The team resisted. The temporary department leader avoided making decisions. The new manager lacked the experience to guide the process. It was like trying to build a skyscraper on quicksand.

By month twelve, we had spent over $100,000 on licensing, implementation, and consulting fees. The result? A system that made everything more complicated and less efficient. When the contract came up for renewal, we cut our losses.

The irony? Six months later, we implemented a solution that actually worked, and it didn't require any new technology. We started with an improved project request form that asked the requestor some critical data points that were previously missing. The form was more of a creative brief than a quick request form. Although we improved the creative intake questionnaire, we kept it simple by using a Google Form to standardize how work was submitted and give the designers adequate guidance.

From there, we introduced a clear approval process that established which requests moved forward and who needed to be involved in the decision-making. To ensure projects were completed efficiently, we set standard timelines based on project type and implemented a service level agreement (SLA). This allowed the team to better plan and manage expectations. A key addition was holding weekly capacity planning meetings, which helped us stay ahead of potential bottlenecks and allocate resources more effectively.

These foundational changes immediately improved how work flowed through the team. In the end, we realized that a new tool was unnecessary. Instead, we were able to use existing systems to support the new processes we had put in place!

As our workflow became more structured and predictable, we reached a point where the biggest challenge was not inefficiency within the team, but rather the ability to coordinate work across a mix of in-house staff, contract designers, and agencies. The process itself was clear, but we lacked a centralized dashboard that allowed external collaborators to access the project list and provide updates. By focusing on refining the process first, we were able to pinpoint the specific gap that needed to be filled, without making a broad and expensive investment in technology.

Once these fundamentals were working, we began searching for a tool that could support our process rather than replace it. This approach allowed us to be highly selective in choosing a solution that solved our exact problem without unnecessary complexity. After evaluating multiple options, we implemented Smartsheet, a flexible platform that allowed us to track project progress, streamline collaboration, and enhance our budgeting dashboard. Some call Smartsheet a glorified Excel tool, and in many cases, it is. But the cost of this solution was less than 20 percent of the original system that had been proposed, and it met all of our needs without disrupting the efficient workflow we had built. This tool provided the right level of structure and flexibility without overcomplicating our process.

The key takeaway from this experience was that technology should enhance a well-functioning system, not serve as a Band-Aid for deeper inefficiencies. By solving the process challenges first, we were able to confidently choose a tool that fit our needs, rather than letting the tool dictate how we worked.

The lessons from this experience were costly but clear. First, technology cannot fix broken processes, and introducing new tools without a well-defined workflow often makes the problem worse. Kim's urgency to find a quick solution led her to invest in technology without addressing the root issues, which only accelerated her departure. The failure wasn't in the tool itself but in the misguided belief that software alone could resolve deeper inefficiencies.

Second, before bringing in any new technology, it is essential to establish a strong foundation and have a clear understanding of what the tool needs to accomplish. A structured, effective process must come first, allowing teams to pinpoint the specific gaps that require technological support. Only then should a tool be selected to enhance, rather than dictate, the way work is managed. The best solution is not always the newest or most advanced system, but rather the one that seamlessly fits the organization's needs and strengthens an already functional process.

On the flip side, when the foundation is solid and the process is clear, technology can be a powerful accelerator.

One of the most transformative tools available today is artificial intelligence (AI). When used correctly, the implementation and use of AI within your team can expand capacity, reduce manual tasks, and enhance the quality of output in ways we couldn't have imagined a few years ago. In the next section, we'll explore how AI can become a force multiplier for you and your marketing team.

AUGMENTED INTELLIGENCE

Remember when we used to flip through the yellow pages to find a business phone number? I do.

Do you remember the day the yellow pages stopped being delivered to your house?

I, for one, do *not* remember. Why? Mainly because I did not miss that book. By then, I, like the rest of America, was using Google or Dogpile or AOL to find phone numbers for businesses instead.

The end of the yellow pages reminds me of a quote by Paul Roetzer, the founder of SmarterX:

"When does your life and career noticeably change to the point where you will look back and think of how things were before and after?"[3]

I believe that we are experiencing this point again with AI. In the next few years, we'll look back and think, *How did we ever get around without AI?* It'll be a nostalgic thought, like remembering the days when we navigated to unknown locations using physical maps and printed directions. Thank goodness for the invention of GPS!

In 2024, I led a project with my team that required large amounts of research, analysis, and recommendations to improve the customer journey for a client. We leveraged AI, and our team saved over 60 man-hours of work by using readily available AI tools. The benefit to the client? We were able to deliver the project recommendations and guide the implementation within a tight six-month timeframe. Without AI, this would have easily been a nine- to twelve-month project.

The project came about with a phone call from the CRO of Harrison Steelworks, Jim, who asked me to help with a problem his team was facing. As the CRO, Jim was responsible for sales and marketing. I met with Jim in his office, and he gave me a quick rundown of his operations.

---

[3]   Paul Roetzer, host, "The Artificial Intelligence Show, Ep. 87: Reactions to Altman's AI Quote, Enterprises Embrace AI Models & How AI Is Changing Writing," podcast, on YouTube, March 17, 2024, 1:16:49, https://www.youtube.com/watch?v=goMG4wz9sn4.

His product was a B2C product, and most of the sales were made in the homes of customers. They had a magnificent lead program, and they had an entire team that would simply schedule meetings for their sales team. They made typical "kitchen table" sales, that is, the type of selling that is done at a customer's home, usually through a conversation "around the kitchen table" while products, colors, features, and pricing are discussed.

He explained how the product worked, then started to walk me through the questions and answers a typical sales rep would cover. As I sat there watching his screen, I was slightly mortified at the questions he had to answer to give me a quote for a typical product. The system was asking all sorts of questions that I'm sure were relevant to the operations of the business, but they were dreadful for the customer. I was floored. What customer wants to sit through this product build-out? I mean, who cares about the number of holes and nails? The only quote I was getting was the one that kept popping up in my mind: "Tell me the time, not how to build the clock!"

Think about it: It's like buying a car. As a buyer, you want to know about the specs, the look, and the cost. You don't really want to know about the intricacies of the fuel tank or the tubes that connect the engine to the rest of the car, right? I'm sure there is a very small percentage of people who care deeply about the pipes and the diameter of each one. But those people probably already know what car they want, which defeats the purpose of selling in the first place. The average consumer just doesn't care.

Well, these questions in the quoting system seemed similar: irrelevant to the customer, albeit critical to the manufacturing team. Like with many clients, this was an urgent project that needed to be resolved within six months.

After outlining the scope and kicking off the project, I moved forward with scheduling a series of discovery meetings and sales ride-alongs over a four-week period. I kid you not, during some of these ride-alongs, the customers would say things like, "While you're doing that, I'm going to jump on this call," or, "Is it okay if I go have my coffee while you finish your work here?" During most of the ride-alongs, I felt like we were overstaying our welcome at the customer's home. An odd feeling, indeed.

Why did we stay so long? Well, most of the time, it was because the rep had to answer thirty questions or more just so they could give the customer a quote.

Beyond sales, I met with multiple other departments, including manufacturing, installation, measuring, purchasing, permitting, project management, customer experience, IT, and business development. The goal was to ensure we gathered input from all the departments that covered the entire customer lifecycle. The interactions were a mix of in-person meetings, phone calls, video conferencing, and numerous email exchanges with follow-up questions.

In the end, we had over eighty pages of notes, a dozen recorded meetings, and numerous business documents that ranged from job descriptions to processes!

The task at hand was to consolidate all notes (written, digital, and recordings); analyze the content and data; and determine trends, bottlenecks, and areas of improvement. Once all the data was streamlined, we could start seeing trends and obvious weaknesses in their system and process. We then needed to outline recommendations for system and process improvements to meet the client's goals. This usually takes a decent amount of brainstorming and experience. My agency also likes to go beyond recommendations and include a high-level cost/benefit analysis and an overview of the prioritization and timing for the recommendations, along with expected results for each item.

Traditionally, this work would have been broken down as follows (caveat: this is a general overview, not an exact step-by-step guide or recommendation):

ANALYSIS AND CONSOLIDATION PHASE (SEVENTY-ONE TO NINETY-FIVE HOURS)

The first phase of the project focused on gathering, processing, and making sense of a vast amount of information to ensure that any recommendations were based on concrete data rather than assumptions. This analysis and consolidation phase would normally require between seventy-one and ninety-five hours and involve multiple layers of review and organization.

The process began with collecting and processing over eighty pages of notes taken during discovery sessions, which needed to be carefully reviewed and synthesized. This was followed by transcribing and analyzing recorded meetings to capture key insights and ensure that nothing was overlooked. Additionally, we conducted a thorough review of business documents provided by the client, which helped contextualize the findings and confirm any operational constraints or opportunities. In short, we had a mountain of paperwork to sift through!

Beyond gathering information, this phase also involved structuring the data in a way that allowed for clear analysis. We built workflows to map out existing processes, highlighting inefficiencies and potential areas for optimization. Initial data organization was a critical step, as it set the foundation for identifying patterns and drawing meaningful conclusions. From there, we categorized findings into key themes, such as emerging trends, recurring bottlenecks, and areas that required immediate attention. This structured approach ensured that every insight was backed by evidence, setting the stage for strategic decision-making in the next phase of the project.

THE BRAINSTORMING AND RECOMMENDATIONS DEVELOPMENT PHASE (SEVENTY-FIVE TO EIGHTY-SIX HOURS)

With a solid foundation of data from the analysis phase, the next step was to translate insights into actionable strategies. The brainstorming and recommendations development phase, which would require seventy-five to eighty-six hours, focused on problem-solving, evaluating potential solutions, and developing a structured plan for implementation. This phase was not just about generating ideas but about critically assessing which recommendations would have the greatest impact and how they could be executed effectively.

Traditionally, the process begins with in-depth analysis and problem-solving, using the findings from the previous phase to identify the most pressing challenges and uncover opportunities for improvement. Each proposed solution undergoes a cost/benefit analysis to ensure feasibility and alignment with business goals. Once viable options are identified, we develop a prioritization approach to determine which initiatives should be tackled first based on urgency, resources required, and potential return on investment. Finally, we compile all insights and strategic recommendations into a structured format, dedicating time to documentation and presentation preparation to clearly communicate findings to key stakeholders. By the end of this phase, we've not only outlined actionable steps but also equipped leadership with a data-backed roadmap for moving forward.

The total time invested in this project would have been 146 to 181 hours.

There is nothing wrong with this approach; it's a common and detailed step that cannot be skipped. However, if there's a more efficient and effective way to do it, why not try it?

It's like refusing to look up a recipe online and instead insisting on doing the work the "old-fashioned" way by either a) driving to the local public library, searching for a cookbook or a book from a specific chef, and flipping through the pages until you find the recipe you want; or b) cooking by trial and error, making up the recipe a few times until you find the right one. Sure, making up a recipe can be fun if you are into cooking and like to experiment. But for the rest of us, if we need a quick recipe to get dinner on the table for the family, we're likely to call a friend or look it up online. It's not an easy "cheat" button; it's an efficient button. Having an easier, better alternative just makes life … well, easier and better.

Similarly, knowing that there is this thing called the "internet" that can give you a full list of ingredients, recipes, and even alternative ingredients, why would you choose *not* to use it?

On that note, I'd like to introduce artificial intelligence: the never-tiring, eager-to-learn-and-do-more assistant. Or as I like to call it, "augmented intelligence." I heard this phrase in a podcast, and I think it's a genius way of summarizing what AI is and does.

For this project, we leveraged AI as we could while ensuring client confidentiality, honoring their personal and business data. Even though we didn't use AI to its full potential, the tools we did use were able to cut our time by roughly 50 percent. In the end, we used a mix of seven different AI tools and platforms to complete this phase in the project. These tools included AI transcription and summaries, initial pattern/trend identification, AI-assisted analysis and brainstorming, and AI-enhanced PowerPoint development. In three weeks, I was ready to meet with the team to review and discuss our initial recommendations for a broader brainstorming session. We leveraged AI to help with a lot of the tedious manual work, and even with some of the initial brainstorming and "bouncing off" of ideas.

It's worth noting here that human time is still needed; it's incredibly important to ensure human experience and expertise are influencing the outcomes. These human touches include quality control and verification, strategic decision-making, client-specific customizations and quirks, expert judgment on recommendations, cost/benefit analysis refinement, and timeline projections. That said, implementing AI can greatly reduce man-hours and even provide a better-quality product.

Here was our final breakdown:

The analysis and consolidation phase was reduced to twenty-two hours. The brainstorming and recommendations development phase was reduced to forty-five hours.

This means a project that normally would have taken up to 181 hours only took us sixty-seven hours to complete. That's a reduction of over 60 percent! And the quality of the end result was better because our team could focus on strategy and refinement instead of starting from scratch.

Now, I know what you're thinking, because I thought it too: *But won't AI replace marketers? Agencies? Creative professionals?*

Sam Altman, CEO of OpenAI, predicts that 95 percent of what marketers use agencies, strategists, and creative professionals for today will easily and nearly instantly be handled by AI at almost no cost.

Sounds scary, right? But remember the yellow pages story? Yes, people lost jobs in phone book publishing, but entire new industries emerged around digital marketing and SEO.

The same thing is happening now. AI isn't replacing marketers—it's transforming how we work. As Dario Amodei, CEO of Anthropic, puts it: "It becomes your coworker; it becomes your personal assistant."[4]

But like any tool, it's only as good as how you use it. Remember that project management software Kim implemented that no

---

[4]   Noah Smith and Erik Torenberg, hosts, "Econ 102 with : Anthropic CEO Dario Amodei on AI's Moat, Risk, and SB 1047," Turpentine Network Podcast on Apple, August 29, 2024, 1 hour 3 minutes, https://podcasts.apple.com/us/podcast/anthropic-ceo-dario-amodei-on-ais-moat-risk-and-sb-1047/id1696419056?i=1000667000126.

one used? The same thing can happen with AI if you don't implement it correctly.

My first attempt at implementing AI with my team at the agency was a disaster. I was so excited about the technology that I tried to enable AI in everything at once. The result? A bit of chaos.

Half of my support team was confused about which tools to use and when to use them. With multiple AI-powered platforms in play, there was no clear structure dictating which one to use. The excitement of automation quickly turned into a headache, as we were forcing the use of various tools that accomplished the same thing.

Content quality also suffered. Without a clear strategy for AI-assisted writing, the messaging lost its natural tone and started sounding robotic. Instead of enhancing our brand voice, the AI-generated content diluted it, making it clear that automation alone was not the solution. What should have saved us time ended up requiring more manual intervention to correct mistakes and maintain brand integrity. In some ways, the team was actually slower because people were struggling with too many new tools being introduced at the same time. It was like giving a student driver the keys to a Ferrari. The power was there, but they were not ready to use it.

Without a structured and phased approach, AI was becoming just another distraction. A couple of months after implementation, I decided to slow down and be more strategic about the tools to introduce and require. I started to think about the tasks that I didn't care for and that took up too much of my time. I posed the same question to my team. Through this lens, we narrowed down the tools that benefitted our working styles, without requiring a complete overhaul of our workflow.

The key takeaway from this experience was that AI implementation should be intentional, not impulsive. It's easy to get caught up in the excitement of automation, but without clear objectives, AI can quickly become a burden rather than a benefit. The goal isn't to force technology into every aspect of work, but to integrate it where it truly enhances efficiency. The more gradual and thoughtful the adoption, the more likely teams are to embrace the change rather than resist it.

If you are implementing AI for a team or department, use the 3-Step AI Accelerator.

Start by focusing on the first three days by selecting only one repetitive process and experimenting with a simple AI tool. Instead of overwhelming your team with multiple changes at once, test the tool yourself, document what works and what doesn't, and refine your approach.

Over the next three weeks, introduce the tool to a small team of two to three members. Gather feedback frequently, ideally three times per week, to understand pain points and refine the process as needed. This is also the time to document workflows and track any noticeable time savings, though measuring impact isn't mandatory at this stage. The goal is to build familiarity and comfort with AI in a low-risk, high-learning environment.

During the next three months, begin scaling the implementation. Each month after the initial phase, expand usage to more teams, add additional features as needed, and start measuring the long-term impact. By this stage, your focus should shift to optimizing processes and planning for the next phase of AI integration based on real-world usage rather than assumptions.

AI adoption is an evolution. The most effective implementations happen when teams understand the purpose behind the tools, see the benefits firsthand, and have the time to adapt without disruption. When used right, AI becomes a true accelerator, not just another experiment in automation.

SOLO IMPLEMENTATION

If you have hesitations about implementing and using AI, you are not alone. Many professionals recognize AI's potential to expedite work but remain cautious about relying on it entirely. It's a valid concern—while AI can enhance efficiency, it cannot be trusted blindly. The key to overcoming this hesitation is to start small and build confidence through controlled experimentation.

A structured approach to easing into AI adoption is what I call the AI Trust Test. This method helps you refine your use of AI tools in a way that feels manageable and effective. True to the theme of working in threes, this test also consists of a three-step approach.

First, take three minutes to clearly articulate your problem or task in writing before using any AI tools. One of the biggest mistakes in working with AI is jumping in with vague or incomplete instructions. Just like in any structured workflow, the quality of the input determines the quality of the output. Taking the time to define your request ensures that the AI tool has a clear directive, leading to more useful responses.

Next, give yourself three attempts to refine your prompt. Rarely will the first attempt produce exactly what you need. Instead of dismissing AI after an imperfect result, adjust your prompt based on what worked and what didn't. Think of it as an iterative process, where each attempt moves you closer to a useful output. Through repetition, you'll quickly learn how to fine-tune AI instructions to get the best results.

Finally, start with only three specific use cases in your workflow. Instead of trying to implement AI across your entire operation, focus on a few tasks where it can immediately add value. These could include generating first drafts of project briefs, reviewing and editing submitted outlines or data, summarizing meeting notes, or drafting memos and emails.

Mastering a few key use cases will build familiarity and trust in AI, making it easier to expand its role over time.

The goal is not to replace critical thinking but to streamline repetitive or time-consuming tasks so you can focus on higher-value work. By gradually incorporating AI using this structured approach, you'll develop the confidence to use it effectively while maintaining control over the quality of your outputs. With time, AI will become less of an unknown variable and more of a trusted assistant in your workflow.

COMMON PITFALLS

Many teams, myself included, have fallen into common traps that can slow down adoption of AI or create unnecessary frustration. AI requires thoughtful implementation, clear processes, and ongoing adjustments to truly deliver value. Based on my own experience, here are three of the most common mistakes and how to avoid them.

The first pitfall is what I'll call the "everything now" trap. In my eagerness to implement AI, I made the mistake of introducing multiple AI tools at once, expecting immediate results. Instead of improving efficiency, this created confusion and slowed down adoption. The better approach is to start small. Focus on one tool, one team, and one process at a time. This allows for controlled implementation, making it easier to refine processes, address challenges, and scale AI adoption gradually.

Another common mistake is the opposite of "everything now:" the "perfect tool" myth. I spent too much time evaluating different AI platforms, believing that the right tool would solve everything. The reality is that there is no single perfect AI solution. Rather than getting stuck in endless comparisons, a smart approach is to pick a good-enough tool, test it, and adjust as needed. AI tools evolve quickly, and what works today may change tomorrow. The key is to stay flexible and prioritize functionality over perfection.

The last major pitfall is the "set and forget" mistake. In my initial AI rollout, I assumed that simply giving my team access to AI tools would be enough. Without proper training or structured onboarding, adoption was slow, and mistakes were made. AI is only as effective as the people using it, so a better approach is to implement structured onboarding, provide ongoing training, and conduct regular check-ins. This ensures that the team understands how to use AI tools effectively and that processes continue to evolve based on real feedback.

Avoiding these pitfalls can make a huge difference between a frustrating AI rollout and a smooth, impactful integration. AI adoption is a continuous process that requires refinement, learning, and adaptation. By taking a measured approach, you'll set yourself up for long-term success rather than short-term setbacks.

If things go wrong (and they will), try not to panic or revert to the traditional ways. Instead, take a pragmatic approach and treat the issue as you would a trialing phase: Gather team feedback or customer feedback, if possible.

Based on the feedback, adjust settings and usage guidelines. To ensure you are properly scaling and testing, I would recommend starting small and internally before using AI on customer- or client-facing content.

The benefits of AI are plenty, but here are a few success metrics to watch and track to help ensure your and your team's time investing in AI is well spent. The first one is time saved on a specific task. This should be measured by actual numbers (hours and minutes), not just estimates.

Other common success metrics are error rates and time to launch. Ideally, the use of AI tools will reduce the number of human errors and the length of time to review and approve a project.

Overall, the introduction of AI should be gradual and produce real results in terms of time savings and quality of work.

Remember these three main points when using AI:

1. Implementing AI is not about replacing human judgment—it's about giving humans better tools to work with.

2. AI is a tool for acceleration. If used in the right way, it can give you 40 to 60 percent of a solution that you can build upon, not a 100 percent solution that replaces human judgment.

3. The data you put in should be legally compliant. In other words, be sure you are appropriately maintaining privacy. Perhaps change titles/names/ data inputs so that you stay in compliance with your company's data privacy policies.

Kim's story is a perfect example of what happens when technology is implemented in a rush without first addressing the real issues. Technology cannot fix broken processes, unclear priorities, or a lack of leadership.

When used correctly, the right technology can help deliver efficiencies and scalability. I have seen firsthand how a simple shift in approach—focusing on process first and technology second—can transform operations.

As a newer technology, AI can significantly reduce time spent on menial tasks, such as transcribing meetings, analyzing data, and drafting reports, allowing marketers to focus on strategy and decision-making. However, AI must be introduced thoughtfully, with human oversight and a clear understanding of its strengths and limitations.

Unlike traditional marketing technology, AI is not just another tool. It is a shift in how we work. It does not replace processes, but it can enhance or help create them.

The following are some very practical tools that I found helpful.

USING KRISP TO AUTOMATE MEETING NOTES, REDUCING OVERLOAD AND MEETING FATIGUE

As a senior leader and executive, you are likely to be in meetings all day. It's a never-ending parade. Sometimes there is even a meeting to discuss the items for an upcoming meeting! And then there's another meeting to discuss *that* meeting. It's a fact of life.

You open your calendar in the morning and see back-to-back appointments. The first is a 7:30 a.m. meeting, so you'll be taking that one in the car or from home. According to your calendar, you have a different topic, conversation, and meeting purpose every hour of the working day. Your 8:30 a.m. is your stand-up with your team. Your 9 a.m. meeting is with your boss, your 10 a.m. is your one-on-one for the week with one of your team members, you're kicking off a project at 11 a.m., and you have a new vendor meeting from 11:45 a.m. to 1 p.m., after which you need to meet with IT to discuss priorities. Your day is a blur of meetings.

On top of that, you wonder if your 11:45 a.m. meeting will include lunch or if you will need to resort to ordering from Uber Eats. And of course, you'll need to ask permission to use the restroom (or announce you're late due to a "bio-break").

Welcome to being a leader in Corporate America. I know many companies are strict with meeting schedules, but eradicating meetings is not possible. Your job is to learn to manage them a bit better.

Depending on the size and culture of your organization, you may have someone assigned to take notes at meetings for you, but that may not always be the case. As a leader, you'll often need to meet with vendors and clients in person. In my case, there have also been times when something was phrased perfectly in a meeting, but later I couldn't recall the exact wording. I also couldn't remember important information and next steps at the end of a long day; there were too many notes to go through.

Now, with transcribed notes, I can easily find the information I'm looking for.

To help with this, I use the platform Krisp for all my meetings. There are other similar tools, but Krisp offers background noise cancellation, which is a non-negotiable for me. Dogs barking, lawn mowers, a loud office neighbor, it's all noise that is cancelled with Krisp.

Krisp also transcribes all notes regardless of platform (Teams, Zoom, Google Meets, etc.). It summarizes the notes and assigns action items, and you can use Zapier to transpose those notes into tasks on your chosen platform. Krisp is also very economically priced, and the free version already gives you most of these features. It's even helped me build outlines from proposals based on scope conversations I've had with clients. Super easy!

Imagine you have wrapped up a meeting, and as it's done, you can quickly see the summary immediately pop up, along with action items.

Depending on your workflow, you can take this information and

1. Send it to your assistant to edit/distribute the notes.

2. Take your action items from the list and add them to your preferred method of tracking your to-do list (Tasks on Outlook, Notes, etc.).

    a. For even greater efficiency, you can take this a step further and leverage AI to automatically build out tasks and reminders based on meeting action items, ensuring nothing falls through the cracks.

3. Quickly scan action items to ensure you have none left, so you can move on to the next meeting.

4. Quickly skim, edit, and send notes off to all the meeting attendees. The output is very sophisticated, so you will see that not many edits are needed.

Previously, I spent over fifteen hours per week in meetings, followed by an additional three hours or more of writing summaries, action items, and next steps. Now, AI transcribes every meeting, generates concise summaries, and automatically extracts action items. As a result, I have recovered approximately ten hours of administrative time each month.

DEFINING PROJECT SCOPES AND TIMELINES: SETTING CLEAR EXPECTATIONS FROM THE START WITH CHATGPT AND CLAUDE

Every project I need to scope starts with a meeting to understand what the work entails or what the problem is. Some clients even bring up new projects while we are meeting about ongoing projects. For the most part, I have a good understanding of their needs, and I can outline what I heard in layman's terms and have them agree or edit it.

But moving this conversation into a formal proposal takes time. I used to spend hours on proposals to ensure I had captured most points, thought about the cost and the approach, etc. Now I write my thoughts and parameters into Claude and ChatGPT and have them spit out a proposal along with estimated timelines. Instead of staring at a blank screen, my starting point is an outline and a scope that is about 70 percent of the way to being complete. This alone has saved me at least three hours for every proposal I send out. In my agency, the outcome is a proposal. In corporate, these would be project scopes. For corporate projects, I can have AI tools outline project plans and estimate timelines, as well as outline the skills needed to drive projects forward.

Another quick win I have found is using Claude or ChatGPT to generate an initial draft using meeting transcripts or notes, which are also collected with AI. My AI tools transcribe the meetings and summarize the notes and action items. With Zapier, this data can then be pushed into the paid subscription of ChatGPT or Claude, and these tools output an initial project scope draft that I can edit and refine.

Once you have an outline of the proposal or project scope, you can then upload it into your PowerPoint AI presentation creator (I recommend Beautiful.AI) and have it produce a presentation that you can use for project alignment meetings or approvals.

There are many other tools available, but some of the most common ones are Claude, ChatGPT, and Gemini. For a full list of some of my favorite tools, you can go to https://bit.ly/ DiggPlaybook.

With AI handling the heavy lifting of drafting project scopes and timelines, your focus can shift from tedious document creation to refining and enhancing the details that matter most. This not only speeds up the process but also ensures greater clarity and alignment from the start. Whether you're in an agency setting crafting client proposals or in a corporate environment outlining internal project plans, AI streamlines the workflow, allowing you to spend more time on strategy and execution.

Now that we've covered scoping and planning, let's move on to how AI can help with brainstorming.

BRAINSTORMING SMARTER: USING AI TO SPARK IDEAS AND IMPROVE CREATIVITY

Have you ever needed to bounce an idea off someone? You've called a colleague, a trusted friend, or a family member with the hope of using them as a "sounding board." You are trying to solve a problem or better articulate your idea. Or maybe you have some ideas on how to solve the problem or launch a product, but you still need to vet out the details. You need to have an open, nonjudgmental conversation to work through some of the blind spots or build upon the initial idea.

The phrase "sounding board" comes from the world of acoustics and originally referred to a flat surface placed behind or above a speaker or musical instrument to reflect and amplify sound. This allowed the speaker's voice or the instrument's sound to project more clearly and reach a larger audience.

Over time, the concept of a sounding board has become a metaphor for ideation and feedback. Just as a physical sounding board helps to enhance and clarify sound, a person or group serving as a "sounding board" helps to reflect, clarify, and refine thoughts, ideas, or plans.

Having a metaphorical sounding board is incredibly valuable, but it's not always possible. Sometimes it's after hours, and you don't want to intrude on your team. Maybe it's late at night or too early for you to have a brainstorming session. Or perhaps your thoughts and ideas are still too premature to discuss with another person.

Here is where AI can help.

Think of AI as a virtual chat with a colleague—your first sounding board.

It might sound strange at first, but think about all the times you needed a sounding board yet couldn't even formulate the right words. Well, now you can get a head start by chatting with a computer program that can help you identify pain points and help you better articulate your starting point.

This can be your sounding board! At the very least, it can help you polish your thoughts before you move on to your traditional sounding board.

You can even prompt various platforms to help you vet out a specific thought or idea. Similar to brainstorming, these tools can be used for strategic or basic problem-solving.

STRATEGIC PROBLEM-SOLVING: USING AI TO IDENTIFY AND OVERCOME CHALLENGES

According to Kidlin's law, a problem-solving theory: "If you write the problem down clearly, then the matter is half solved." This simple but powerful theory is rooted in the idea that if you write down exactly what your problem is, then your thoughts around the problem will become clearer and more organized. As a result, solutions will become more apparent, and you will eventually find a solution.

My take on this is to use a generative AI tool to help you put Kidlin's law into practice. You can use a tool like ChatGPT, Gemini, or Claude to write your problem into a prompt and ask the system to help you solve said problem (by giving it the right parameters, of course).

By writing this prompt and thinking clearly about the problem you are trying to solve, you are already in a better position than you were before using AI—and that's even before you've hit send!

AI will *not* give you the exact right solution, but it still makes for a decent sounding board. These modules are advanced enough to assist you in narrowing down to the solution you have in mind or vetting out solutions that might not work.

Think of these platforms as chatbots, but with broader searching intelligence and access to expanded capabilities. You can also think of AI as you would Google: It can serve as a robust, and much more improved, search engine.

For example, if you are looking to buy a midsize SUV under $40,000 that can seat eight people, AI will give you a few models and outline the pros and cons for each one.

Meanwhile, if you Google it, you'll mostly get a list of paid advertisements that aren't necessarily the most relevant results.

Clearly, AI is much more accurate and helpful.

Similarly, you can use AI to help you advance your thoughts and ideas. Whether you're writing an email, a memo, a blog post, or ad copy, AI can give you a rough draft or optimize your current content.

You can also include a short summary of your target audience and have AI help you alter your writing so that it performs better. Next time you start to write anything, consider pushing it through AI for a quick clean-up or first draft. With some tools, you can even upload your company tone and voice to ensure the content is on brand.

I've used AI tools to help me build focused plans and strategies for building my business, understand why I have not won a client proposal, and even find mistakes (and areas for improvement) in my marketing. It's been a phenomenal problem-solving aid for me. But so far, my favorite benefits of AI have been the time savings and the ease in developing powerful PowerPoint presentations.

FROM BLANK SLIDES TO STUNNING DECKS: USING AI POWERPOINT DEVELOPMENT TOOLS

It was 5:45 p.m., and most of the employees had gone home. I was an assistant, working with the executives on the PowerPoint presentation for their five-year plan. Most of the document was a template, but there were a few places where we were allowed to take the liberty to customize the slides. I was in the boardroom presenting on the projector that would be used for the meeting. The CEO was adamant about seeing the presentation using the same projector and screen size so we could see the same colors and charts. This would ensure the presentation was up to standard.

This CEO—we'll call him Bob—was a stickler for excellent presentations. He had very strict guidelines we had to follow. Many of us learned this lesson the hard way. In one meeting, an engineer was presenting updates on a product's development. Bob stopped him in the middle of the presentation and said:

"I can read faster than you can talk. I do not need you to read slides to me! Either tell me something that is not on the slides, or don't bother presenting the slide."

It was a harsh and embarrassing lesson. That day, we all learned that titles had better tell a story.

As you can see, reviewing presentations with Bob was an uncomfortable experience. It was now around 6:30, and I was tired and ready to go home. On one slide, Bob said, "That line is crooked."

"It's a straight line."

"No, it's a crooked line. Zoom in."

I zoomed in to about 400 percent, and sure enough, Bob was right. That darn line was crooked.

These lessons taught me the importance of visual communication in PowerPoint. Sometimes I can explain something better on a slide than in an email.

Despite my appreciation for PowerPoint, I would sometimes dread having to put together slides for every meeting. While I knew the story I needed to tell or the information I needed to share, sometimes the visuals wouldn't come to me. I'd waste time searching for old slides that I could reuse or even search online for inspiration. At times, I'd even work with someone to convey my thoughts and have them put together slides for me. We once paid a company to help us tell the story of a brand merger through visual concepts. They did a phenomenal job, but it cost us a few thousand dollars and many man-hours to meet with them and build the slides. I've even tried using templates and various other PowerPoint alternatives. Some were adequate, but most fell short of their promises.

I did, however, find a golden nugget that claims—and I can confirm this—that their platform saves most of their users about 40 percent of their time. It is Beautiful.AI, an AI presentation development platform, and it's mind-blowing. Here are a few scenarios I've used this tool for (while building presentations for my clients' project deliverables). For ease, I'll outline each type of scenario with almost the exact wording I used in the AI.

- Platform launches using a similar script to the one below:

- You are a marketing director that is launching a marketing tool that will be used as the digital asset management platform for the company. You need to build a PowerPoint that will be used to introduce this tool to the marketing team and sales team. The benefits of this tool are ABC. The timing for launch is X, and the support will include XYZ.

- Product pricing changes:

  - You are the sales VP and you need to communicate the product pricing strategy and changes to the sales teams. These pricing changes include moving away from BOM-based pricing and instead using a mix of product hierarchies, market demand, and business profit goals to determine pricing. You need to include a high-level summary of the new pricing strategy and how this will benefit the sales team.

- Change management:

  - You are leading the change management efforts for the project of a system improvement and change. The outside sales team will be working with an "inside sales team," allowing them to focus more on client sales and less on the administrative side of selling. You need to outline a PowerPoint that explains the change, the benefits, and the risks we've outlined.

Each time, the platform gives me a phenomenal starting point, including charts, graphs, and visuals that would otherwise take me hours to create. The ability to use AI for PowerPoint creation has saved me at least fifteen hours per month.

I've used Gamma, Canva, and a few other options, but I always come back to Beautiful.AI. You can customize its colors and templates to your brand colors, and you can find a good starting point in their templates, but my absolute favorite benefit is the AI generator. You can write in plain English anything you want to convey on a PowerPoint, and it will do an excellent job of putting together five to ten slides on your topic.

Truly, this is a time saver that helps tell the right stories.

Disclosure: You must read every word it puts together and edit for accuracy. Otherwise, you may inadvertently launch a made-up product! The cost is less than your monthly coffee budget, and the outcome is top-tier. When used right, this tool will give you a great starting point for any presentation!

Like all things in life, Beautiful.AI has some constraints. It's a bit fidgety to extract a file into a PowerPoint or other editable file. When this is done, the file loses some of its well-designed layout. The tool also has limitations in customizing the slides, such as formatting text and recreating tables. I also found great limitations in data importing. Basically, this tool is not appropriate for heavy data and report outputs.

With AI-powered tools like Beautiful.AI, the days of spending hours formatting slides, aligning text boxes, and second-guessing visual choices are gone. Instead of struggling to create engaging, professional-looking presentations from scratch, AI helps structure the content, generate relevant visuals, and optimize slide layouts in a fraction of the time.

Of course, while AI can handle the heavy lifting, human oversight is still essential. The technology might give you a polished starting point, but it's up to you to refine the messaging, ensure accuracy, and tailor the slides to your specific audience. Oh, and some of these tools will limit some usage: for example, I cannot find how to change the text color on some texts to highlight as "needs improvement" or "needs to be checked." But these minor inconveniences are worthwhile trade-offs for the time saved on creating a full deck.

Whether you're crafting a strategic pitch, rolling out a major change, or presenting data to executives, AI transforms PowerPoint creation from a tedious task into an efficient, creative process.

QUICK REALITY CHECK

As powerful as AI has become, it's important to recognize its strengths and its limitations. While AI can significantly improve efficiency by handling repetitive tasks, analyzing large sets of data, and generating first drafts, it isn't a replacement for human expertise. The true value of AI comes from knowing when to rely on automation and when human intuition, creativity, and decision-making are essential.

Think of AI as an assistant or a highly efficient employee. It can organize information, identify patterns, and even generate ideas, but it still requires human oversight to ensure accuracy, add context, and make the final call. Understanding this balance is key to leveraging AI effectively without losing the critical human elements that drive strong decision-making and meaningful connections.

What AI does well:

- Routine tasks (meeting summaries, basic research, etc.)

- First drafts and first edits

- Data analysis

- Pattern recognition

What humans do better:

- Strategic thinking

- Creative direction

- Relationship building

- Final decisions

THE IMPORTANCE OF HUMAN OVERSIGHT IN AI-GENERATED WORK

A client of mine runs an engineering firm, and in early 2024, he hired a bright, eager new graduate named Billy. Billy was enthusiastic about applying everything he had learned in school and was excited to contribute to real-world projects. However, as any experienced engineer knows, the transition from academia to practical application is steep. In this firm, junior engineers are typically assigned small tasks within larger projects, with each step meticulously reviewed by a senior engineer before being finalized.

In one case, Billy submitted a set of calculations for review. Immediately, the senior engineer noticed something was off. When asked to explain his methodology, Billy admitted that he had used an AI tool to generate the calculations. The AI had confidently provided him with a research paper reference, but upon closer inspection, it turned out that research paper did not even exist! The numbers were completely fabricated. Had this not been caught, the project could have moved forward based on entirely false data.

On another occasion, Billy was assigned to write a final project report. To make the process easier, the firm provided him with clear templates, reference materials, and guidelines for structuring his work. He completed the report surprisingly quickly and submitted it for review. At first glance, the report was well written, but something about the language did not align with the company's usual tone. As my client read further, he realized that the report was filled with misleading conclusions, overly definitive statements, and technically incorrect recommendations. Clearly, it had been written with AI.

For example, the report described a material as "failing" when in reality, the observed damage was well within the acceptable range of the manufacturer's warranty. The AI-generated language lacked the careful disclaimers and conditional phrasing that engineers use to account for variables. Instead of presenting the nuanced, fact-based assessment that was required, Billy's report sounded definitive, almost like a courtroom ruling rather than an engineering evaluation. Without human review, this report could have led to major misinterpretations, costly mistakes, and a potential hit to the firm's credibility.

AI SHOULD ACCELERATE YOUR EFFICIENCY

These examples highlight why AI should be used to accelerate work rather than replace human judgment. While AI can assist with drafting reports, analyzing data, and identifying patterns, it cannot fully grasp the context, industry nuances, or professional standards that experienced engineers—or professionals in any field—develop over time.

Again, AI is a tool, not a substitute for expertise. It can speed up processes, but human oversight is essential to ensure that outputs are factually correct, contextually appropriate, and aligned with industry standards. As Billy learned, blindly trusting AI can lead to critical errors, but using AI as a starting point paired with human review can enhance efficiency without compromising accuracy.

This is why integrating AI into workflows must be done thoughtfully. The best results come when teams leverage AI for routine tasks while ensuring that the final analysis, decision-making, and critical thinking remain firmly in human hands.

KEY TAKEAWAYS

Technology alone cannot fix broken processes. Introducing new tools without a well-defined workflow often amplifies inefficiencies rather than solving them. Before implementing any new technology, the focus should be on optimizing existing systems to ensure that automation enhances rather than complicates operations.

AI is a powerful tool, but it is not a replacement for human intelligence. While AI can automate tasks and improve efficiency, it lacks the strategic thinking, creativity, and decision-making abilities that humans bring to the table. The key is to use AI to streamline work, not to replace critical thinking.

The best tools are those that your team will actually use, not necessarily the most sophisticated ones. In order to successfully integrate tools into your marketing engine, you must first fix the process, then find the technology that supports it. AI, automation, and smart workflows can save you hours, but only if implemented with clear objectives and proper execution.

Technology will continue to evolve at a rate that we cannot even fathom. These advances will change and improve the way we work, but marketing is still, at its core, a human function. Data, tools, and automation can optimize efficiency, but creativity, strategy, and emotional intelligence drive true marketing success.

Let's explore the human side of marketing and how to balance automation with the irreplaceable power of people.

THE IN-HOUSE VS. OUTSOURCE FORMULA

Get this right, and you'll multiply your impact. Get it wrong, and you'll either waste resources or, worse, lose control of one of your most strategic assets.

Resource allocation will always be a constant challenge in marketing leadership. No matter how large or well funded your team is, there will always be more priorities than bandwidth.

I've seen this in organizations that have a $17 million budget and in those that have no budget at all. They each face the same fundamental challenge: a lack of resources, whether in people, budget, or specialized skill sets. Even in large teams, gaps exist. And when working solo or with a small team, outsourcing and prioritization become survival skills.

AMY'S DILEMMA

The leadership team at TitanForge, a fast-growing manufacturing company, was celebrating its recent acquisition. Outwardly, Amy also smiled and high-fived colleagues. On the inside, her heart raced so loudly that it muted the celebration around her.

Amy was leading a marketing team comprising herself, a marketing generalist, and two specialized agencies.

TitanForge's growth efforts were centered around acquisitions, and with every new acquisition came a new logo, a new website, and a whole new mess of marketing materials, all of varying quality. What should have been an exciting phase of expansion quickly turned into a marketing nightmare. Sales teams were frustrated by inconsistent messaging and a lack of sales materials. Customers were unsure of product offerings, and the leadership team could not understand why Amy's team couldn't produce faster.

And the small marketing team? They were drowning.

The marketing team was caught in a familiar but frustrating predicament: too many projects, too little bandwidth. Most projects were abandoned midway through so they could make room to support the newest acquisition. Amy found herself drafting the communication pieces for customers (not one of her strengths), only for them to be criticized and sent through endless rounds of revisions. She would review the work of her marketing generalists, only to find numerous mistakes in the details of the product imagery (the generalist was more of a content specialist and less of a creative designer). And she would constantly expand the scope of the work for the agencies (from SEO and website building to developing case studies and brochures). The team had minimal wins and a mountain of complaints.

Brand consistency and strong messaging were critical to positioning the company as an industry leader. But with a limited budget, hiring a full in-house creative team was out of the question. And relying solely on agencies? Too expensive, too slow.

She'd seen this before. She'd even lived it. Amy had personally experienced the thrill of a hiring spree, when budgets were approved and the workload justified it, only to face the gut-wrenching reality of laying off the same people when budgets tightened and the workload dipped.

She could already picture it: Those full-time hires would start looking like a fixed expense the company couldn't afford. That "urgent need" for a creative team? It would fluctuate greatly. Busy one quarter, slow the next. Suddenly, they'd have a full-time team without enough work to justify their salaries. Marketing leaders would then scramble, wondering, "When can we cut this overhead?"

Amy wanted to avoid this headache by building a marketing team that could scale with the business. One that was nimble, efficient, and built for the long haul.

The gaps to fill included strong creative services and support in content creation, so she could focus on the marketing strategy and better manage her specialized agencies.

In order to build a scalable team, Amy needed to determine which roles were core to the business and best kept in-house, which ones were flexible and could be in-house or external, and which ones were highly specialized and best outsourced.

To determine where each role fell, she used a framework to guide her decision. You can use this framework when determining how to scale your team as well.

For each potential role, she systematically answered each of the following questions using a 1–5 scoring scale (1 low, 5 high).

- **Strategic Importance** – Does this role directly impact long-term marketing strategy? The more impactful the role is, the higher the rating should be.

- **Frequency of Need** – Is this an ongoing requirement, or just an occasional high demand? High frequency means a higher score.

- **Internal Expertise** – Does the existing team already have the skills to handle it? If internal alignment with skills is high, then this should be a high score.

- **Cost Efficiency** – Is hiring in-house more cost-effective than outsourcing? If it is, give this a higher score.

After applying the scores, add them all together. The sum of your scores will tell you the best approach to building your team.

If the sum falls between 16 and 20 points, you should look into building an in-house team of fulltime hires.

If the score falls between 11 and 15 points, then a hybrid approach will work best.

For a score of 10 points or lower, you should outsource.

Decision Guide for Capabilities Scoring:

- 16–20 points: In-house

- 11–15 points: Hybrid approach

- 0–10 points: Outsource

Below is a replica of the capabilities scoring system from Amy's dilemma:

Capabilities Scoring Example for Creative Services		
Category	Creative Services	Scoring out of 5
Strategic Importance	Maintaining a strong brand presence was critical for future growth and sales (customer acquisition). A score of high importance was assigned.	5/5
Frequency of Need	The demand for creative assets was high, spanning digital ads, website updates, sales collateral, and trade show materials. While the demand would fluctuate, the ongoing need and maintenance justified a score of 4, fairly high.	4/5
Internal Expertise	The existing designers were not marketers nor designers by trade or education. They were mainly administrative support who picked up odd jobs to help. Overall, the team lacked experienced designers who could execute at scale. A low score was assigned.	2/5
Cost Efficiency	Outsourcing everything would be very expensive, leading to a low score.	2/5
	Total Points	13

The total score was a 13, pointing to a hybrid approach, a blend of in-house and external resources.

Knowing this was the best path forward, Amy carefully considered her options for structuring the team.

One option was to hire a junior designer or freelancer. This was the most affordable choice, but it came with significant trade-offs. A junior hire would need close oversight, which meant Amy or another marketing leader would have to spend time managing them instead of focusing on strategy. There was also the risk of inconsistent branding, since a less experienced designer might struggle to maintain the right tone and quality across multiple projects. A junior designer would also have limited experience and might not have the versatility required to work on different projects.

Another option was to rely on multiple freelancers. This would allow the team to produce a high volume of creative work without committing to a full-time salary. However, it also meant juggling multiple contractors, each with their own style, availability, and learning curve. Managing them all would take time, and without a strong internal point of oversight, maintaining a cohesive brand identity across assets would be a challenge.

The final option was to hire a senior designer, someone with both the creative expertise and strategic vision to own the brand's visual identity. Ideally, this would be someone who could flex down to design when needed, almost like a player-coach.

This approach would meet the needs of strategic importance, frequency, and internal expertise. This was the most expensive choice up front, but it came with long-term advantages. A senior designer could ensure consistency across all assets, reducing the risk of brand dilution. They could also take on the role of managing external freelancers, giving the marketing team the ability to scale up creative production without sacrificing quality. And whenever creative work was minimal, they could do the design work and scale down.

Amy hired a senior designer for the in-house team to take ownership of brand consistency and ensure that every piece of creative work followed a unified style. This role was not just about producing assets but also leaning into the support of the creative direction of the company. Meanwhile, a network of specialized freelancers was brought in to handle execution-heavy work, including social media graphics and production-heavy layouts. This setup allowed the team to remain agile, scaling up or down as needed without the burden of carrying a full-time in-house creative team.

It didn't take long for the results to validate the approach.

Costs were lower than hiring a full in-house team or relying entirely on agencies, giving the marketing department more budget flexibility. Brand consistency was strengthened because the senior designer provided clear direction, ensuring that every asset aligned with the company's visual identity. The marketing output increased since the new hire was able to give structured guidance to freelancers. The marketing generalist was able to focus on communications (taking this off Amy's plate) while reducing the need for endless revisions. And Amy was able to better direct her specialized agencies. All team members were working in their "genius" zone and meeting the business needs.

By committing to a hybrid approach, the marketing team struck the right balance between control and scalability. They kept strategic creative leadership in-house while leveraging external expertise for execution. This allowed them to be nimble, adaptive, and cost-effective. Most importantly, this approach freed up budget and resources for higher-impact initiatives, ensuring that the marketing team wasn't just keeping up with demand but actively driving the business forward.

COMMON PITFALLS TO AVOID

One of the most common pitfalls in outsourcing is delegating strategic capabilities to external partners. While outsourcing execution-heavy work can be a great way to scale, handing off high-level strategic decision-making can weaken the marketing team's ability to drive long-term success.

Core strategy, customer insights, and positioning should remain in-house to ensure alignment with the company's broader business goals.

Another mistake is underestimating management overhead. Hiring freelancers or agencies can seem like a time-saving solution, but managing multiple external partners can quickly become chaotic and too much for one person to handle. A structured approach is required to effectively manage this. Without clear expectations, detailed briefs, and strong internal oversight, outsourced work can lead to misalignment, inefficiencies, and endless revision cycles and can end up being a costly venture. In order to avoid this, clear direction, regular check-ins, thorough quality control, and ongoing cost management are required to ensure work meets expectations.

Without structured processes for feedback and alignment, outsourcing can become inefficient, leading to time-consuming revisions and unexpected costs that offset the intended benefits.

On the flip side, while it's tempting to be the sole strategist and delegate only the production work, this can lead to burnout and bottlenecks. A well-balanced team should have a mix of strategic leaders and executional support.

Another commonly overlooked factor is cultural fit. Even with the best technical skills, external partners who don't align with the company's values, communication style, or workflow can create friction. Agencies and freelancers should not only produce quality work but also integrate smoothly with the internal team, making collaboration seamless rather than a constant struggle.

Finally, technology dependencies can easily be missed in the outsourcing process. Certain marketing functions require integration with internal systems, such as CRM platforms, analytics dashboards, or content management tools. If outsourced partners lack access or experience with these systems, it can create inefficiencies, delays, and data silos. Before outsourcing, it's essential to assess whether the external team will have the necessary tools and knowledge to operate within the company's existing infrastructure.

TIPS FOR SCALING YOUR TEAM

Scaling a marketing team effectively requires careful planning, structured processes, and ongoing evaluation. Here are some quick but critical best practices to keep in mind:

- **Start with one capability at a time.** It can be tempting to overhaul your entire team structure at once, but scaling too quickly can lead to confusion, inefficiencies, and budget misalignment. Instead, start by outsourcing or hiring for one key capability at a time and measuring the impact before expanding further. For example, if design work is causing bottlenecks, hire a freelance designer first rather than bringing on an entire creative team.

Once that process is running smoothly, assess whether additional roles are needed before making further investments.

- **Document processes thoroughly.** Every successful scaling strategy is backed by clear, repeatable processes. Whether you're hiring a new in-house team member or onboarding a freelancer, having documented guidelines ensures consistency and efficiency. These should include project briefs, training material (loom videos, user manuals, etc.), brand guidelines, approval workflows, and communication tools and protocols. The more structured your processes are, the less time you'll spend correcting errors and managing misaligned expectations.

- **Stay flexible.** The needs of your marketing team will fluctuate, so contracts with freelancers and agencies should be designed with flexibility in mind. Avoid long-term commitments unless you're confident that the workload will remain stable. Including scope flexibility clauses allows you to scale work up or down as needed, ensuring that resources align with business demands. Clearly defining expectations on deliverables and timelines helps minimize miscommunication and unnecessary revisions. By structuring contracts this way, your team can pivot quickly if business priorities shift, preventing unnecessary expenses and ensuring agility in your operations.

The reality is that your projects and goals will require some capabilities that you may not have in-house. And justification for these sophisticated roles as an additional full-time headcount may not be feasible. When this happens, do not make the mistake of turning your team into a group of generalists and stretching them beyond their expertise. This approach will likely lead to burnout and a frustrated team.

When you find yourself in the inevitable situation of having to scale, the model Amy used should help you determine what skills to build in-house and which ones to outsource.

Knowing this, you can then focus on building a network of reliable freelancers and agencies that will help you achieve better results at a lower cost than building internal capacity.

THE EVOLUTION OF A SCALABLE TEAM

Your marketing team will evolve over time based on your organization's needs and growth. Having a clear framework, like the one discussed in this chapter, on who to keep in-house and who to outsource will help you make the right decisions for your business.

Here's how this progression can look:

- **Stage 1: Solo Marketer** (No budget, proving impact)
  - Core: You (strategy and management)
  - Flex: Two reliable freelancers
  - Scale: Agency relationships
  - Support: Intern
- **Stage 2: First Real Team** (Budget secured, adding key hires)
  - Core: You and digital marketing manager
  - Flex: Project coordinator/specialist/manager
  - Scale: Agencies for execution
- **Stage 3: Growth Phase** (Building scalable systems)

- **Pod System**: Digital team, operations team, channel team
- Each team has the following members:
    - A strategic lead
    - Core team members
    - Flex resources

Keep in mind that this is just an example of how growth can look; it's not the only way to grow. And the timing for each stage can look very different. You may stay in a certain stage for a few years before the organization evolves to the next one. This is totally normal.

SUCCESS METRICS TO TRACK

Tracking the right success metrics is crucial to ensuring your team, whether full-time, freelance, or a mix of both, is operating efficiently and driving real business impact. These key performance indicators (KPIs) will help you measure effectiveness, identify areas for improvement, and make informed decisions about scaling your team.

COST PER DELIVERABLE

Understanding how much you're spending per completed project or asset is essential for evaluating efficiency. This metric helps determine whether in-house resources, freelancers, or agency partnerships are the most cost-effective for different types of work. For example, if a single social media ad costs twice as much through an agency compared to an in-house designer, you may need to reconsider your allocation of resources.

To measure this, track the total spent on salaries, freelancer fees, and agency costs, then divide this total by the number of deliverables completed in a given period. Be sure to factor in hidden costs, such as time spent on revisions, internal approvals, and communication overhead.

TIME TO MARKET

Speed matters. A well-structured team should be able to produce high-quality work within an acceptable timeframe. If deliverables are consistently delayed, whether due to bottlenecks in approvals, freelancer availability, or inefficiencies in the process, that signals a need for restructuring.

Compare the turnaround times of different workstreams. Are full-time team members quicker at completing some tasks? Are freelancers taking too long because they require excessive back-and-forth communication? Setting clear benchmarks for project completion will help ensure deadlines are met and marketing initiatives stay on track.

QUALITY SCORES

Fast and cheap work is meaningless if it doesn't meet quality standards. Develop a scoring system or feedback loop to assess the quality of deliverables from internal and external team members. This can be as simple as a rating scale from 1 to 5 based on factors like accuracy, creativity, adherence to brand guidelines, and stakeholder satisfaction.

Solicit feedback from key stakeholders, like sales teams, department heads, or clients who rely on these assets. If freelancers or agencies produce high-quality work but require extensive revisions to meet expectations, it might be worth reevaluating the team structure or providing clearer briefs up front.

TEAM SATISFACTION

A highly productive team is also a satisfied team. Whether experienced by full-time employees or freelancers, burnout and frustration lead to turnover, lower-quality work, and inefficiencies. Conduct periodic check-ins or anonymous surveys to gauge workload balance, communication effectiveness, and overall job satisfaction.

For freelancers, this could mean evaluating whether they feel properly briefed, fairly compensated, and aligned with the company's expectations. For full-time team members, it may involve assessing whether they have the support and tools needed to succeed.

SCALABILITY METRICS

A major goal of outsourcing or expanding a team is to ensure work can scale without breaking existing systems. Ask yourself: Is the team able to handle increased demand without excessive overtime or stress? Are workflows structured in a way that allows for seamless expansion? Are external partners flexible enough to scale up or down based on workload?

Tracking the percentage increase in completed projects over time, the ability to absorb additional work without delays, and the smooth onboarding of new hires or freelancers will indicate whether your structure is built for long-term growth.

KEY TAKEAWAYS

Marketing functions can be categorized into three areas:

- Core (must have in-house) – Strategic, business-critical roles

- Flex (can be in-house or external) – Functional expertise that is frequently needed

- Specialized (best outsourced) – Highly specialized or surge-demand roles that don't justify a permanent full-time hire

Use the following capabilities framework to determine which roles to keep in-house and which to outsource. This framework is applied by answering each of the following questions using a 1–5 scoring scale (1 low, 5 high):

Strategic Importance – Higher impact on long-term marketing strategy = higher score

Frequency of Need – High frequency = higher score

Internal Expertise – High internal alignment with skills = higher score

Cost Efficiency – In-house hiring is more cost-effective than outsourcing = higher score

- 16–20 points: In-house

- 11–15 points: Hybrid approach

- 0–10 points: Outsource

Structure your team with the right balance of strategic roles and execution specialists roles. As the sole strategist, it is easy to become overwhelmed and ineffective if key functions are stretched too thin.

Your role as a leader is to structure, prioritize, and drive scalable impact by using the right balance of in-house and outsourced roles. By aligning your team structure with business priorities and leveraging both internal and external talent, you can create a scalable system that delivers results without unnecessary overhead.

In the next chapter, we'll explore how to expand resources with traditional methods.

BEYOND THE ORG CHART: HOW TO SCALE WITH INTERNAL ALLIES AND EXTERNAL EXPERTS

I had just answered a question from an executive in the boardroom when the silence crashed down like a physical weight. Twelve eyes locked on me, unblinking, as my words hung in the air between us.

I was in front of the executive team, presenting our marketing plan by outlining how we would manage multiple product lines, multiple regions, and an aggressive growth target. I had rehearsed my talking points, anticipating the usual budget and strategy questions, but I hadn't prepared for the question that followed.

One of the executives leaned forward and asked, "So, who's handling all of this?"

I hesitated for a beat before answering, "As an FTE, well … just me."

The silence that followed was immediate and heavy. It was the kind of silence that could either mean I had just said something brilliant or something incredibly naïve. I saw a few raised eyebrows, a couple of exchanged glances. Then someone finally broke the silence: Wait, you re the only person working on this? That cannot be right.

I quickly explained that while I was the only official full-time marketing employee, complete execution included strategic partnerships both inside and outside the organization. I laid out how our success would be dependent on collaboration, resourcefulness, and investing in the right external support. We couldn't afford to operate like a traditional marketing department, but we also couldn't afford not to deliver results.

What gave me confidence in this approach was the momentum we had already built. The previous year had been a success, and there was a high level of trust in my ability to deliver. I had created an ecosystem that functioned like a well-structured marketing department, even if we didn't have the headcount to match.

When I first stepped into this role, the reality was simple: I had no formal team. No direct reports, no dedicated specialists. Just me, a blank slate, and a long list of high-stakes marketing needs. But within six months, I had built a support system that rivaled much larger marketing departments.

I started by leveraging internal colleagues. I identified key people in other departments who had the skills or capacity to support marketing initiatives. This included a network of internal partners who helped push projects forward in their areas of expertise. One of my most valuable partnerships came from IT: I borrowed a project coordinator who turned out to be phenomenal at marketing operations. What started as a temporary collaboration soon became an essential part of keeping our marketing efforts organized and efficient.

Beyond internal resources, I expanded externally. I formed relationships with agencies that were true partners and functioned as an extension of our team rather than just vendors. I brought in freelancers and contractors strategically, including a brilliant freelance designer who deeply understood our industry and could execute with precision.

And then there was the intern—hungry to learn, eager to contribute, and more capable than many entry-level hires I'd seen in the past. She quickly became a valuable asset, taking on tasks that freed up my time to focus on strategy and execution at a higher level.

On paper, I was still a team of one. In reality, I had built a marketing operation that was lean, effective, and adaptable. By tapping into the right mix of internal allies, external partners, and fresh talent, we were delivering results that exceeded expectations.

This wasn't a traditional team structure, but in a fast-moving, resource-constrained environment, it was exactly what we needed to thrive.

One of the first steps I took when I needed to build a scalable team, with no budget, was to look at internal partnerships and resources. This approach helped me with some capacity while also allowing me to build strong internal relationships.

CROSS-DEPARTMENT SUPPORT

When I started my marketing career, it was because someone took a chance on me. This path was partly made possible by my curiosity and a willingness to venture beyond my job description, but it was also due to the bravery of a colleague who needed marketing support.

Fresh out of college with a business economics degree, I landed at a corporation that recognized my eagerness to learn and supported my exploration. I started in finance, diving into month-end reports and re-forecasts, even traveling to Canada on a monthly basis to work with the team there. But something felt off.

The cyclical nature of finance work, the frantic rush to close the books followed by weeks of analyzing what the numbers meant, felt like being on a corporate yo-yo. On one particularly memorable Fourth of July, while my U.S. colleagues were celebrating, my boss and I were in the office closing the month

(I wore flip-flops in quiet protest). When the finance work eventually transferred to another office, it felt like a blessing in disguise.

This led me to explore other areas of the business. I worked in customer service handling credits and rebills, then moved to supply chain, where I ended up managing plant inventory and supervising the dispatch team. Each role taught me something new about the business, but I kept finding myself curious about our marketing department's work. Why did they launch certain products? How long did it take to see the impact on the bottom line? This curiosity eventually led me to ask if I could help with any marketing projects, just to learn more about the department.

That's when a colleague, who would later become one of my closest friends, took a chance on me. She asked me to help with pricing analysis for a product she was managing. I was so excited, I could hardly wait to finish my regular work to start on her project. While my initial calculations weren't correct, her patience in teaching me the right approach only fueled my interest more. For me, this "pro bono" work was a chance to test-drive marketing and build experience for my resume. For her, it was free support on a project she needed help with. This arrangement led to more marketing projects on the side, and eventually, a full-time position in the marketing organization. A true win-win that launched my marketing career.

This experience taught me a valuable lesson: There are often talented people within your organization who are interested in learning about marketing, just as I was. They might be

- looking to expand their skill set,

- interested in a career change,

- curious to understand how different departments work, or

- seeking new challenges beyond their current role.

Having colleagues who directly benefit from a project you're working on is one of the most valuable yet overlooked sources of free support. These individuals have a vested interest in the project's success, which means they are often willing to contribute in ways that can help you move faster and gain internal traction. Their involvement can help lighten the workload, and it can also improve the project's visibility and long-term success.

One of the most impactful ways colleagues can support your project is through *sponsorship*. A well-placed internal sponsor can influence leadership, advocate for your project's importance, and help secure necessary approvals or budget allocations. Having a sponsor in your corner elevates the project's priority level, making it easier to gain buy-in from decision-makers.

Beyond sponsorship, colleagues can also provide *tangible resources* to support execution. This could mean dedicating their own time to assist with specific tasks or even allocating members of their team to help move things forward. Whether it's a subject matter expert offering insights or an operations team assisting with logistics, tapping into internal resources can fill gaps that might otherwise require external hiring or additional budget to outsource support.

Finally, never underestimate the power of *moral support and informal feedback*. Sometimes, the most valuable contribution a colleague can make is about perspective. Whether it's spot-checking a key deliverable, reviewing a presentation before you bring it to leadership, or serving as a sounding board for refining your pitch, these moments of informal collaboration can sharpen your work and increase your confidence.

By recognizing and strategically leveraging internal resources, especially those that neither have a marketing degree nor work in the marketing department, you can turn internal allies into powerful partners, ensuring your project gains momentum without relying solely on formal resources.

One way to look for and leverage non-marketing resources is by outlining what type of project and skill sets you are looking for. Below are four steps you can take that will help you identify what projects would be adequate for support from non-marketing resources, as well as tips for how to identify these resources.

The first step is to **identify potential projects** or tasks that you need to get done and that don't solely require marketing expertise. In the past, this has included tasks such as offering support in coordinating meetings, taking notes, and following up with action items. Here are some other examples that fall into this category:

- Data analysis

- Graphs and reports build-out (or dashboard)

- Event planning and coordination (including administration or behind-the-scenes)

- Research projects

- Content creation and management (with a highly specific strategy and approvals)

- Project coordination

The second step is to **identify internal colleagues** who can potentially support your projects. Be open-minded about this. Do *not* eliminate employees from consideration simply because *you* think they have no interest or because they do not have marketing experience. You may be pleasantly surprised!

Here are some starter questions to help you choose potential colleagues:

- Who will benefit from the implementation of this project? Many of my projects get support from other departments who realize certain project implementations will actually support *their* teams (e.g., IT, finance, customer service).

- Who is at the junior level in their career and open to trying out new projects or learning about new departments?

- Who has some capacity and is willing to help another department?

Now that you have a list of potential projects and a short list of potential resources, the third step is to **set clear parameters** on the type of support you will need. Make a list detailing the project scope, support needed, expected time commitments, potential learning objectives, and success metrics. This will ensure clear communication of what you are looking for.

For project scope, write out the purpose of the project and what success looks like. List what is in and out of that scope. Then outline the specific support you need—for example, if you need help building a dashboard, include samples of dashboards and preferred platforms (Excel, Power BI, etc.). Having this all outlined will make approaching your colleagues for support easier.

Once you have this information, you can start vetting your colleagues and discussing their capacity and potential interest in supporting your marketing project.

After a colleague has agreed to support you on a project, the final step is to ensure that you **create a support structure** so that you can provide sufficient support and feedback. Treat your colleague like you would a regular teammate and schedule regular fifteen-minute check-ins. These meetings will ensure the project progresses at the right pace and stays on track. Offer access to training materials and platforms if necessary, and provide ample feedback.

Leveraging internal resources from other departments provides ample benefits to you, the company, and your colleagues. At face value, marketing gets additional support. Your colleagues gain valuable experience. And you support potential cross-functional career growth and strengthen overall team relationships between departments. Everyone wins!

While there are a variety of benefits to this approach, there are also some things to watch out for. Mainly, the work may not be done, it may be delayed, or it may be done incorrectly, like I did when given my first pro bono marketing assignment. In order to account for these issues, you will need to allocate extra time for your project to be completed. This is so you have time to correct the work, request revisions on it, or, worst-case scenario, do it yourself.

For example, let's say Deliverable X is due on March 11, so you might ask your colleague to complete their portion by March 1. You'll have ten- to fifteen-minute weekly check-ins to measure their progress. They can ask any questions they have during these meetings, so they don't need to ambush you while you're busy with your own work. If they're on track, great! If they're struggling, however, you don't need to panic, because you'll still have ten extra days to fix any mistakes and help them complete the project. (Additional actionable steps on how to implement this approach can be found in Appendix D and at https://bit.ly/DiggPlaybook.)

ADDITIONAL BENEFIT OF CROSS-DEPARTMENT COLLABORATION

While talent development is one aspect of internal partnerships, there's another equally important dimension: collaborating with other departments on shared initiatives. This was highlighted in what I call "The Olivia Story."

Olivia was a senior marketing manager at Caine Manufacturing. She had identified a need for a new digital asset management (DAM) platform and work management tool that could also serve as a project management software. On paper, this was a marketing project. In reality, it would impact multiple departments, mainly the project management office (PMO) and IT.

Olivia made a critical mistake: She didn't involve other departments in the decision-making process. She signed the contract for an enterprise-level feature that required buy-in from IT and the PMO. When she finally arranged a demo for leadership, opinions were divided. Some didn't see the value, while others couldn't commit the necessary resources required for the implementation of the tool. The project ultimately failed, and the organization had to write off the deposit and initial payments as a sunk cost.

In short, the project failed because Olivia hadn't built the right cross-functional partnerships.

To avoid this costly mistake, Olivia should have approached this as a collaborative initiative rather than a marketing-only project. She needed to build relationships with the IT and PMO leaders early in the process, understanding their constraints, priorities, and perspectives. By involving these stakeholders from the beginning, she could have gained valuable insights, addressed potential objections, and secured the necessary resource commitments before making any financial obligations. Most importantly, she should have created a shared vision of success that aligned with the goals of all departments involved, ensuring everyone saw value in the implementation and felt ownership of the outcomes.

To ensure you do not make a similar mistake, there are three main points you need to consider. First, identify stakeholders early. Successful cross-functional projects begin with a thorough stakeholder analysis. This means identifying everyone who will be impacted by the project, whose support will be critical for implementation, and who possesses valuable expertise that could enhance the project's outcome. Taking time for this crucial step prevents the oversight that doomed Olivia's initiative.

Next, build relationships before you need them. This involves maintaining regular check-ins with other departments, genuinely understanding their challenges and goals, and finding opportunities to support their initiatives. These investments in relationship building create goodwill and trust that become invaluable when cross-functional cooperation is needed.

Finally, and perhaps most importantly, ensure that collaborative projects offer benefits to all involved departments. This means clearly articulating how the initiative supports each team's objectives, determining what resources each department can realistically contribute, and establishing metrics that measure collective success rather than departmental wins. When everyone sees their interests reflected in a project, commitment naturally follows.

WORKING WITH EXTERNAL PARTNERS

While internal partnerships are crucial, sometimes you need specialized expertise or additional capacity that can only come from outside your organization. This section will explore how to effectively work with agencies, freelancers, and other external partners to achieve optimal results.

THE AGENCY SELECTION PROCESS: FINDING YOUR PERFECT MATCH

Think of finding the right agency like dating—you'll likely have to kiss a few frogs before finding your prince. It might feel like you are on a hamster wheel of first dates full of the typical boring questions like "What do you do for fun?" I've been there, you've been there. It sucks.

Fortunately, unlike dating, you can streamline the process of finding an agency with a structured approach that respects everyone's time and increases your chances of success.

RUNNING EFFICIENT INTRODUCTION MEETINGS

Preparation and structure are critical! Before you even start scheduling agency meetings, take forty-five minutes to prepare an "agency introduction deck" (maximum of ten slides). Below is a quick cheat sheet of what to include in this deck (bonus points if you use AI to help you build the deck and cut your time to twenty-five minutes!):

- Slides 1 and 2: Your organization's overview and culture

- Slides 3 and 4: Current challenges and opportunities

- Slides 5 and 6: Specific needs and project scope

- Slides 7 and 8: Success metrics and timeline

- Slides 9 and 10: Budget range and decision criteria

Once your deck is built and you start reaching out to agencies, schedule thirty- to forty-five-minute meetings and set the agenda:

- First five minutes: Intros and agenda setting

- Next fifteen minutes: Your intro presentation

- Following fifteen minutes: Agency capabilities and open conversation on their thoughts and questions following your specific needs and scope

- Final ten minutes: Next steps and timeline

Pro Tip: Never schedule sixty-minute introduction meetings. They tend to become unfocused and often don't provide additional value. Instead, I recommend thirty to forty-five minutes max.

Evaluation Criteria: Create a standardized scorecard for evaluating agencies. Rate every agency across the scorecard, and if you have multiple stakeholders, also have them evaluate each agency after every meeting. You can find a sample scorecard to use in Appendix D and at https://bit.ly/DiggPlaybook.

SETTING UP FOR SUCCESS: THE FIRST NINETY DAYS

The first few months of any agency relationship are crucial. This is when you set the foundation for success—or plant the seeds of failure.

We once hired what seemed like the perfect agency. Great portfolio, solid experience, competitive rates. The project seemed straightforward: We needed to understand our brand's equity in the marketplace—how customers perceived us, what they valued about our brand, and where we stood against competitors. The agency had done similar work for other large companies, and their forty-five-day timeline seemed aggressive but doable.

Two weeks in, it became painfully clear something was wrong. While we wanted a comprehensive brand equity study that included competitive analysis and market positioning, the agency was narrowly focused on customer satisfaction surveys. During our first review meeting, they presented a plan that basically asked us to hand over our customer list so they could run basic satisfaction questionnaires. No competitive context. No market positioning. No deep dive into brand perceptions. And when we tried to course-correct, the problems only multiplied! Our first review meeting revealed a fundamental misalignment. The agency simply presented a plan to collect basic satisfaction scores using our customer list, with no competitive context, market positioning analysis, or deep dive into brand perceptions.

The agency was unaware of our internal strict approval compliance requirements, proposing to contact customers directly without the appropriate internal approvals. We had failed to establish clear success metrics; while we sought actionable insights about our market position, they focused solely on delivering raw satisfaction data. Their staffing choices further highlighted the disconnect. They assigned junior researchers when our needs demanded experienced brand strategists capable of extracting meaningful insights from the data.

Most critically, we hadn't cultivated the necessary relationships. Their account team approached this as a routine customer survey rather than the strategic brand initiative we envisioned, and they neglected to engage with our senior stakeholders, whose guidance could have significantly improved their approach.

Six weeks and several frustrating meetings later, we had to fire them. Not because their work was bad—they were actually quite good at what they did—but because what they did wasn't what we needed. We had failed to clearly articulate our expectations and ensure they understood our real objectives before signing the contract. It was an expensive lesson in the importance of proper agency onboarding and alignment. Ensure the above items are discussed and understood, and if it's not a right fit, end the relationship. Do not try to salvage a partnership that won't work.

This story illustrates why proper onboarding and alignment are crucial. Here's what we should have done differently:

1. Clearly defined success metrics up front

2. Established approval processes during week one

3. Confirmed team structure and expertise alignment

4. Set up proper stakeholder engagement protocols

In the Appendix D, I've included a checklist for successfully setting up an agency relationship.

CRISIS PREVENTION AND MANAGEMENT

I was the brand marketing director at a large corporation ($2 billion in annual revenue) and had recently been promoted to another division. This new division used the same agency I had previously worked with, so I thought this would be an easy transition. It wasn't.

The dynamic between my new team and the agency—which we'll call "The Fire"—was rocky. Deadlines were continuously missed, scopes were always growing and changing, and communication was inconsistent. Overall, not a great working relationship. At one point, I ended a call early because team members from both teams were getting too rude and starting to insult and blame each other for the lack of production.

The Fire and our company had been working together for two years, so I was shocked to see how this relationship had deteriorated.

A few months after I abruptly ended that meeting, the president of The Fire, "John," planned to come down to meet with some of our leaders. By this point, these visits were routine for us. Over the years of working with The Fire, I had developed a professional relationship with John and his right-hand woman.

As we usually did, John and I had dinner the night before his visit to our company. We went to one of my favorite restaurants in Tampa, and because this was a friendly dinner, my husband joined us. We had a great meal and a great conversation that included some business talk. After this dinner, my husband and I were convinced that The Fire was going to fire us as a client.

The next morning, before John came into the office, I met with my boss and gave him a heads-up. My boss was adamant (to the point of being arrogant) that we would not be fired as a client. He was so convinced that we bet on it: If The Fire fired us, my boss owed me an expensive lunch. If not, the meal was on me.

After that meeting, my boss bought me lunch.

The reason we were fired was our team's unprofessionalism. As a client, we were costing them money, and their team was not happy working with us. I do not blame The Fire; if anything, I applaud their bravery. The lesson here is that my boss and John could have had better communication and prevented the teams from descending into a toxic relationship. As for me, I probably should have been more stern and forceful in mitigating the relationship when I saw how toxic it had become.

THE LESSON

Sometimes, despite everyone's best efforts, relationships can become strained. Here are the early warning signs to watch for:

- Missed deadlines without proactive communication

- Scope creep without proper documentation

- Team members showing frustration in meetings

- Decrease in work quality

- Lack of proactive ideas and engagement.

My boss should *not* have been surprised to be fired, and our team should have been more courteous. On the flip side, The Fire should have allowed for some time to remedy the situation. Perhaps a good "Come to Jesus" session with all team members would have been worthwhile. Of course, I was new to this team, so I do not know what conversations previously took place.

Open and honest conversations about work production, the team's support, and the overall relationship are crucial. If one party wants to "fire" the other, it should not come as a surprise. Treat your agencies like you would your employees: Give them a chance to make things right.

Agencies can be powerful partners, but success requires more than just choosing the right one. Your agency should become an extension of your team, not just a vendor. I've had great experiences with agency partners where they've even been able to help us spot weaknesses in our team.

SEEING THE FOREST FOR THE TREES

While I was working at Rockwell & Sons Manufacturing, we had gotten to a point where the marketing team was growing. I had gone from a team of one to a team of six. My peers (other VPs and directors) had increased from five to about ten, and we now had a CMO (previously, the highest marketing title was VP). Our team had more than doubled in size, and so had our marketing budget.

One of the newer hires was a director in the marketing department. Stacy was well-spoken and smart. Yet, I heard rumors of her style: She was a bit too abrasive and, at times, mean to those in a lower position. I had not personally experienced any of this, nor had my team complained. But the rumors that she was tough to work with and for persisted.

After a few months, I got a call from an agency we had been working with. I had worked with this agency for a few years and was very familiar with their leadership. This time, the president called my cell phone. The conversation went something like this:

"Hi, Joselyne! So good to catch up with you! How's your team? Seems like you're adding new members."

"Hi, Mike! Yes, the team has exploded! I'm now overseeing marketing operations; it's been stressful sometimes, but so much fun overall! How are things on your end with the projects you all are managing for us?"

"Well, that's what I wanted to talk to you about. Do you work much with Stacy?"

"Not directly, no. Why?"

"Well, my team has complained several times about her behavior. She's been yelling and insulting people during meetings. Has she done anything like that to you?"

"No, but I've heard rumors that she can be a bit … abrasive."

"Joselyne, we've been working together for a long time, so I'm going to be blunt with you. My team does *not* want to work on any project she's assigned to. I've tried reaching out to her boss, but he doesn't return my calls or emails, and I don't want to have to take this to the CMO. To be honest, it's hard to believe Stacy works for your organization and no one else has experienced this behavior."

"I hear you. I'll nudge Stacy's boss to give you a call. He really needs to hear this."

"Thank you. We've had such a good working relationship over the years; I can't believe your culture has changed so much. I'll give Stacy's boss another buzz, but please know that after this project, my team will not work with your company if Stacy is involved."

"Thanks for the heads-up, Mike. I'll talk to Stacy's boss too. Hopefully you two can have a productive conversation."

The key takeaway from this scenario is how quickly toxic behavior can damage external partnerships and internal team dynamics. While rumors circulated about Stacy's abrasive management style, it took an external partner threatening to cut ties with the company to force leadership action. Shortly after this conversation, Stacy's boss removed her from her position and put her through "management rehabilitation." He tried to help her, but in the end, Stacy was fired over the same complaints he'd been getting from the beginning.

LESSON LEARNED

Your agency partners have a great outside perspective and will give you some nuggets of information and points of view that you may not see because you are too close. Those partners make money from your efforts, so it is in their best interest to ensure you are successful and continue to grow.

When an agency partner takes the time to have uncomfortable conversations with you, like the one Mike had with me, you should listen and dig deeper into the issue they are bringing up. Chances are you are too close to the trees to see the forest.

Hiring agencies as a flex for your capacity is a traditional method to help you scale. I've employed this method in almost every company I've worked in, and you probably have too. Most of my experiences have been great, with a few outstanding memories (and a few head-shaking, I-can't-believe-that-just-happened moments). When you find an agency that truly understands your business, communicates effectively, and delivers consistently, they can become an invaluable strategic partner.

THE FREELANCE PARTNERSHIP: BUILDING YOUR DREAM TEAM, ONE EXPERT AT A TIME

They called me the "Queen Contractor," and not always as a compliment.

We had a massive product launch coming up—you know, the kind that keeps you up at night and makes you question every decision. The traditional playbook said we needed to hire a full-time designer. It made sense on paper. We had the budget. We had the workload. It was the "responsible" choice. But something didn't feel right.

Although hiring a full-time designer would give me enough flexibility to fully control output, it would also limit my output to only creative work. Yes, we needed sophisticated creative work, but we also needed more than that. We needed strategic design thinking for the brand elements. We needed someone who could crank out daily social media assets (copy and infographics), and we needed technical illustrations that would make our engineers proud. It was clear that I needed a variety of skill sets usually not found within a single creative designer. That's when it hit me: We didn't need one person trying to be everything. We needed the right people at the right time, and we needed them doing the right things.

So, I did something a little unexpected. I had the budget and approvals for a full-time hire—an opportunity most leaders would have taken, as increasing headcount would allow them to increase their budgets. Instead, I brought in three freelancers: a senior content and marketing strategist who could see the big picture, a production designer who could make things happen fast and be billed per project instead of per hour, and a technical illustration wizard who could turn complex specs into beautiful visuals.

The cost was about the same as one full-time hire, but the impact was so much greater!

Our launch was transformative. Each freelancer brought their specific expertise exactly when we needed it. No square pegs in round holes. No asking someone to be good at everything. Just pure, focused talent aimed at specific challenges.

Now, before you think this is a catch-all solution, let me tell you about Sarah, a contractor I once hired only to quickly regret it.

Sarah was what I call my "expensive lesson" in freelance hiring. On paper, she was perfect. She was a freelance project manager with twenty years of experience and a track record of successful website launches. In reality? She was a masterclass in how the wrong cultural fit can turn your office into a war zone.

Cultural fit is about alignment with your organization and existing team. It's about how well a person's attitude and work style mesh with an organization's unwritten rules of interaction. It doesn't mean hiring copies of existing team members but finding individuals who can thrive within your company's unique ecosystem while contributing diverse perspectives. Even the most technically qualified candidate becomes a liability when unable to adapt to organizational cultural expectations. And Sarah's rigidly formal approach directly conflicted with our culture.

It was Sarah's third day, and she was running her first meeting at the company. But by her attitude, you would have thought she was commanding a military operation. At one point, a VP tried to ask a question about the timeline, and Sarah—I still cringe thinking about this—actually told him to "hold all questions until the designated Q&A portion of the meeting."

The room went so quiet, you could hear people's careers flashing before their eyes.

At this company, we prided ourselves on fostering a collaborative environment, where open dialogue was not just encouraged but essential to our success. Our leadership team had cultivated a culture where ideas flowed freely across hierarchical lines, and even junior team members felt comfortable raising concerns or offering suggestions.

Sarah's military-command style couldn't have been more at odds with this ecosystem. That moment with the VP was only the tip of the iceberg.

In meetings, Sarah would abruptly cut people off mid-sentence if their updates were taking too long and going past their allotted time. She refused to allow any challenges to the project plan because they would "slow down the work," effectively shutting down valuable input that might have prevented later issues. The collaborative discussions that had been our company's lifeblood were suddenly replaced with rigid, one-way briefings.

Outside of meetings, Sarah's approach was equally jarring. She would relentlessly nag team members for updates on action items, sometimes multiple times a day if she didn't receive an immediate response. Her impatience manifested in terse emails and abrupt hallway conversations that left team members feeling more like subordinates than valued contributors.

The effects rippled through the organization quickly. Team members began avoiding her, withholding concerns about the project because they dreaded the battle it would take to get a word in edgewise. Several VPs and directors simply stopped attending web meetings altogether, unwilling to subject themselves to an environment where they weren't permitted to speak unless formally presenting.

Perhaps most concerning was how Sarah's approach began undermining the project itself. Critical decisions needed to be made, but the team had no pathway to the free-flowing brainstorming sessions necessary to work through complex problems.

In just one month, Sarah had achieved something remarkable: She had united our entire organization in the shared belief that she needed to go. She'd managed to turn simple status updates into endurance tests and basic feedback sessions into war negotiations.

Was she technically competent? Absolutely. Did that matter in the end? Not one bit.

That experience changed how I work with freelancers. It taught me that technical skills are only table stakes. Now I look for more than that:

- Adaptability: Can they read the room? Adjust their style? Work within our culture?

- Communication style: How well do they communicate?

- Problem-solving approach: Do they bulldoze through issues or navigate around them?

- Cultural intelligence: Can they work with different personalities and levels of the organization?

Remember that senior designer I mentioned earlier, from the product launch? She's still my go-to person fifteen years later. When she's not available, I'll actually move project timelines to wait for her. Why? Because over the years, she's become a trusted partner who does the background work needed to learn my clients' businesses. She is highly adaptable and can adjust to various work cultures.

These days, when people ask me about working with freelancers, I tell them to think of it like building a great restaurant's contact list. You need to know a few amazing specialty suppliers who might not be there every day, but who will deliver exactly what you need when it matters most. When you find those rare gems, hold on to them. Build relationships with them. Treat them like the valuable partners they are.

Having a network of trusted freelance partners allows you to easily flex your team with the right talent at the right time. You'll be able to scale up or down as needed, and you'll know that when you really need something done right, you've got someone you can count on.

These reliable partners become invaluable as they learn your business inside and out, developing a nuanced understanding of your industry challenges and organizational goals. They come to understand your culture, adapting to your communication style and work processes without the friction that comes with constantly onboarding new talent. Over time, they build genuine relationships with your team members, creating smoother collaborations and more efficient workflows.

Perhaps most importantly, these seasoned freelancers can hit the ground running on new projects, bypassing lengthy orientation periods and delivering quality work from day one. When you consider all these advantages together, a roster of trusted freelance talent truly is worth its weight in gold.

In the appendix, I've included an outline for building your freelance "dream team," including many of the processes I still employ today.

THE INTERN OPPORTUNITY

Marketing leaders often fall into the trap of thinking they need experienced professionals to grow their team. I certainly did. As a marketing leader reporting directly to the CMO, with a "team" that consisted of just me and a few agencies, I was drowning in work. But what I really needed wasn't another senior strategist or a seasoned manager.

I needed someone who wouldn't come in with preconceived notions about how things should be done, but who would bring fresh eyes and genuine curiosity. I needed someone who was hungry to learn and willing to start from the ground up. And most importantly, I needed someone who could take the numerous small but crucial tasks that were eating up my day off my plate.

As I weighed my options and the type of support I needed, I realized that about 30 to 40 percent of my day was spent on tasks that required minimal experience but maximum attention to detail: updating spreadsheets with invoice information, tracking POs and bills, gathering competitive intelligence, and formatting presentations. These weren't strategic responsibilities that justified my salary level, yet they were essential to keep our marketing operations running smoothly.

I decided to hire an intern, believing they would approach these tasks with enthusiasm rather than viewing them as burdensome. They would bring digital native skills and recent academic knowledge that might introduce innovative approaches to our established processes. The cost-effectiveness was also a nice perk. Additionally, I saw an opportunity to develop my own leadership skills by mentoring someone early in their career, which would strengthen my management credentials.

Perhaps most compelling was the potential to cultivate talent specifically shaped to our organization's needs. Unlike experienced hires, who might resist adaptation, an intern would absorb our culture, processes, and expectations from day one, potentially becoming a perfectly tailored full-time team member down the road.

The interview process was eye-opening. Some candidates came in practically demanding a full-time offer before they'd even started. Others seemed more interested in the company's benefits package than the opportunity to learn. But then I met Emma.

She walked in wearing a dark blue suit that looked like she'd borrowed it from an older sister's closet. Her long blonde hair and bright blue eyes contrasted with the formal attire, making her look like a kid playing dress-up in Corporate America. When I asked about her strengths, she paused thoughtfully and said, "Interviewing. I've done so many of these interviews. I think I'm good at it, but I haven't found a job yet, so maybe not. I don't know what my strengths are because I still have to prove myself, but I do know I really want to work in marketing, and I'll do any kind of job just to be in the industry."

Her honesty was refreshing. No rehearsed answers about being a "perfectionist" or "working too hard." Just raw authenticity and genuine hunger to learn. I hired her on the spot.

Emma turned out to be transformative for our team. She brought an eagerness to learn that translated into meticulous attention to detail. She wasn't afraid to ask questions, but she also took initiative. When we later added a digital marketer to the team, Emma's foundation in our processes helped accelerate their onboarding. Together, they became a powerhouse duo that accomplished more than I could have imagined.

Emma's success wasn't just about her abilities. It was about matching the right level of responsibility with the right stage of career development. Too often, I see companies hiring interns as a Band-Aid for senior-level gaps, setting both the intern and the team up for failure. They bring in college students expecting them to act as experienced generalists, then wonder why their internship program isn't delivering results.

DETERMINING IF AN INTERN IS RIGHT FOR YOUR TEAM

Before you start your intern search, you need to honestly assess if your team can benefit from and properly support an intern. Is this the right component to add to your engine? Consider these questions:

- Do you have enough structured, learning-appropriate tasks to fill an intern's day during their internship? Remember, you can structure the internship with as much flexibility as you and the intern need.

- Are you or your team spending significant time (more than five hours a week) on routine tasks that could be delegated?

- Have you tried delegating menial tasks to an AI tool? If not, can an intern try to build out a process leveraging AI?

- Do you have a backlog of data entry or research projects gathering dust?

- Is there a long list of content needs that aren't being met?

- Do you experience seasonal spikes in workload during trade shows, events, campaigns, or product launches?

Make sure your team can dedicate time to proper training and mentorship. Ask who will manage and support this intern. Many interns have never worked in an office setting and will need substantial guidance. Make sure you've assigned the right mentor or supervisor for their success and to ensure your goals and projects are executed properly. Consider how much time can realistically be dedicated to teaching and oversight before selecting a supervisor.

Also ensure your expectations are aligned with entry-level capabilities. Interns are inexperienced, so you need to be careful not to give them work that requires strategic thinking and extensive experience. A common pitfall is expecting too much from an intern.

Will this internship provide genuine value to both your team and the intern's development? Every project you assign should pass a simple litmus test:

- Can the task be broken into clear, manageable steps?

- Is there adequate time for training and supervision?

- Will the project provide meaningful learning opportunities?

- Does the timeline align with the internship duration?

- Is there low risk if mistakes are made (which they likely will be)?

These are some tasks that an intern can excel at:

Research and Data Collection: Interns can excel at gathering and conducting basic analysis of digital metrics (social media performance, search trends, website analytics), market research (industry trends in colors, materials, or other relevant areas), and customer insights (buying patterns, frequently asked questions from customers and sales teams).

Content Organization: From maintaining content calendars to cleaning up digital asset management systems to organizing portal categorization, interns can bring fresh eyes and energy to the organizational tasks that established team members often put off.

Administrative Support: While not glamorous, scheduling tasks, coordinating meetings, and documenting processes are valuable skills for interns to develop that also provide essential support to the team.

Event Support: Interns can manage name tags, logistics, registration, attendee communications, and post-event surveys for feedback, giving them exposure to the full lifecycle of event marketing.

Data Entry and Reporting: Tracking KPIs, inputting data, and summarizing results can provide interns with valuable insights into marketing measurement while taking time-consuming tasks off your plate.

Basic Design and Editing: Content development drafts, simple graphic support, and PowerPoint editing or rough drafting can allow creative interns to contribute to the team while building their portfolios.

Internships can be excellent sources of support that also help develop future talent. Building an effective intern program follows similar principles to hiring freelancers and contractors. Below is a thorough breakdown of steps to take to find an intern who will be a good fit:

Structure the Program: Create a clear job scope with defined deliverables. What will the intern work on? What projects will they support? What skills and responsibilities will they inherit from this internship?

Include concrete learning objectives, goals, and measurable performance metrics. Make sure to establish regular check-ins and feedback sessions throughout their time with the company, and ensure proper supervision and support during the internship. Assign a dedicated mentor who is invested in the intern's success and who will offer regular constructive feedback, establish clear communication channels, and create growth opportunities for the intern.

Create a Professional Job Posting: Before posting your internship opportunity, develop a comprehensive job description. Your company likely has a template, but if not, include these essential elements:

- **Title and basics:** "Marketing Intern" with location (office or remote), hours (part-time or full-time), compensation (hourly rate or unpaid), and duration (semester, specific date range, or number of months)

- **Company introduction:** A brief description of your organization and why you're seeking a marketing intern

- **Responsibilities:** Specific tasks the intern will handle, from social media content creation and market research to organizing digital assets and tracking metrics

- **Requirements:** Educational background (typically pursuing a degree in marketing, communications,

PR, or a related field), necessary skills (Microsoft Office, social media familiarity), and personal qualities (attention to detail, communication skills)

- **Benefits offered:** Hands-on experience, mentorship opportunities, potential for future employment, networking connections, and schedule flexibility

- **Application instructions:** Clear guidance on how to apply, what materials to submit, and any deadlines

Finding Qualified Interns: Once your posting is ready, target your search effectively:

- **Local Universities and Colleges:** Research nearby educational institutions and connect with their career services departments, campus job fair coordinators, and relevant department heads (marketing, business, communications).

- **Professional Associations:** Organizations like the American Marketing Association often have student chapters and can connect you with motivated marketing students.

- **Professional Network:** Post this intern opportunity on your LinkedIn as a post, or reach out to your network via email and direct messages to let them know of this job posting. Get creative; I've even seen interns looking for internships on Facebook neighborhood groups!

- **Personalized Outreach:** Send out direct messages about this position, and be sure to highlight the specific experiences your internship offers, the support structure you provide, and why students would benefit from working with your organization.

THE RETURN ON INVESTMENT

Emma's story isn't unique. When structured properly, internship programs deliver tremendous value to organizations while providing invaluable experience to students. Beyond the immediate productivity gains, interns bring fresh perspectives, current academic knowledge, and digital native skills that can revitalize marketing teams.

I've seen many successful hires begin as interns, having already absorbed our culture, learned our processes, and demonstrated their capabilities before joining full-time. The mentorship experience also strengthens your leadership team, giving rising managers valuable experience in training and development.

While establishing an effective internship program requires investment, the returns in productivity, talent pipeline development, and fresh thinking make it a very smart addition to your marketing engine.

KEY TAKEAWAYS

In summary, building a scalable team in marketing involves strategically leveraging various resources. By combining internal partnerships, external expertise (freelancers and contractors), agency support, and interns, even a team of one can operate like a department of many.

Leverage internal colleagues through effective internal partnerships. Identify those who benefit from your marketing projects and enlist their support in a mutually beneficial way. Foster cross-functional collaboration by recognizing colleagues across departments whose success is tied to your marketing initiatives, then develop talent through knowledge sharing and joint projects that create value for all involved.

Freelancers provide flexible expertise when you need specialized skills or temporary capacity. Instead of hiring full-time staff for temporary or specialized needs, consider using freelancers with clear scope and deliverables. This approach allows you to scale up or down quickly, access niche expertise, and maintain budget flexibility while building relationships with reliable partners who understand your business.

Choose agencies wisely, understanding that not all agencies are the right fit for your organization. Ensure cultural alignment, clear expectations, and defined communication processes to avoid misalignment and wasted resources. Engage agencies strategically for specialized expertise and large-scale projects where their infrastructure and collective capabilities deliver value beyond what individuals can provide.

Interns offer scalable, budget-friendly support when properly structured and managed. With clear roles and proper mentorship, interns can bring fresh energy and contribute meaningfully to marketing efforts while developing their skills. Bringing in interns for entry-level support provides fresh perspectives and helps build your talent pipeline for future growth.

The key is building strong relationships, maintaining clear communication, and setting well-defined expectations across all partnerships. By leveraging these various resources, you can create a marketing engine that delivers results beyond your headcount.

Having established the frameworks to build your scalable team, it's time to pivot to the crucial next step of your leadership journey: demonstrating clear value to earn your seat at the table of strategic discussions. In the next chapter, we'll explore how to translate your team's capabilities into organizational influence and secure that seat at the decision-making table.

PROVING YOUR WORTH

All the pride I had in our accomplishments evaporated, replaced by a sinking realization that I might be nothing more than overhead to the company.

For years, marketing teams have struggled with the same challenge: proving their impact on business results. It is not enough to be busy. It is not enough to complete projects on time.

I learned this the hard way when I walked into a quarterly review.

As marketing director, I had just implemented a new digital asset management system, rolled out updated sales materials across all regions, and finished a successful sales/marketing meeting. The team had worked incredibly hard. We'd delivered everything on time and under budget. I walked into my quarterly review feeling great.

That feeling lasted exactly three minutes, until my boss asked one simple question: "What was the business impact?"

I started talking about project completion rates, efficiency gains, and team productivity. He cut me off: "No, what was the impact on revenue? On market share? On customer acquisition?"

I had plenty of marketing metrics, but I couldn't directly tie our work to business results. That was the day I learned a crucial lesson: In marketing, doing good work isn't enough; you have to prove that work is good for business.

At that moment, I felt the ground shift beneath me. The months of late nights, the careful coordination, and the celebration of our on-time project completions suddenly felt hollow and meaningless. I questioned whether I had been pouring my energy into vanity projects that looked good in marketing presentations but did nothing for the bottom line.

The weight of this realization was crushing. In the span of a three-minute exchange, I went from feeling like a successful director to feeling like an expensive liability. My mind raced through all our recent projects, desperately searching for the business connections I should have been tracking all along. The silence that followed my boss's question felt deafening as I confronted the uncomfortable truth that I had been acting as a project manager, efficiently checking boxes and meeting deadlines, when I needed to be thinking like a business leader, focused on moving critical metrics forward. That day changed not just how I approached my role but how I defined success in marketing altogether.

With this feedback, I went back to my data. I realized I had been tracking almost every metric imaginable, and while it did make for an impressive dashboard, it was still hollow. My dashboard included social media metrics, website analytics (every possible number), email statistics (open rates, click rates, you name it), content performance, project completion rates, team productivity stats, and a budget tracker.

My team and I spent hours compiling this data every month. I had created beautiful charts and graphs that I was so proud of. But I couldn't find the metrics that tied our work to results for the business.

I took a step back and forced myself to find the metrics that mattered while still maintaining our other marketing data. My team and I picked key numbers:

1. 1. Marketing-influenced revenue (what the executives cared about)

2. 2. Sales cycle length (what the sales team cared about)

3. 3. Leading and lagging metrics

Everything else became supporting metrics. Want to know if social media is working? Great, I have that data! And now I can show you how it impacts those key numbers.

In marketing, you will lead and run many projects, from social media campaigns to events. The "completion" of these projects cannot be the only metric of success, nor should they be the only metrics you discuss. Even delivering on time and under budget is not good enough.

To make matters worse, you will also run into many colleagues and leaders who believe marketing is simply overhead and not necessary. You will need to change your mentality and align your projects to specific business outcomes and goals.

Various metrics can be used to discuss business outcomes. Your responsibility is to find the key metrics that matter the most to your business and measure your efforts against those. Here are a few examples of work that is usually completed by a marketing team and how you can talk about these projects in business terms:

Traditional	Business-focused goal
Implementing a new digital asset management system	30 percent reduction in sales cycles because reps can find materials faster
Rolling out updated sales materials across all regions	$200,000 of annual savings in content production costs
Sales/marketing meeting that delivered key initiatives to impact spec share	Two-basis-point improvement in our specification share
LinkedIn engagement increased by 50 percent	LinkedIn leads are converting 30 percent faster than other sources, reducing our average sales cycle by fifteen days

If these metrics are not readily available, start collecting the data necessary to set a baseline (see below). Once your baseline is set, you can adjust your goals to say your team will improve said baseline by a certain number of basis points.

Below is a brief summary on how to start collecting this information. (Note: This is a very detailed section in the book that you may want to let one of your supervisors or managers handle instead.)

Start with sales conversations by scheduling meetings with your sales leaders to understand their process. Ask specific questions:

- "How long does it typically take to close a deal?"

- "What marketing materials do you use most often?"

- "Where do you lose deals and why?"

Document their answers to establish rough benchmarks. Implement basic tracking systems by beginning with simple tools you already have: Use Google Analytics to track website visitor paths, add UTM codes to your campaign links, create basic landing pages for specific initiatives, and set up conversion tracking in your email platform. Remember, the goal is to collect consistent data that relates your efforts to sales.

Create simple feedback loops by asking sales to flag deals that involved marketing content. Have customers complete quick surveys after purchases, track which content pieces are being downloaded, and monitor how often sales teams access marketing materials. Build your historical context by looking back at the past six to twelve months of sales data. Document when major marketing initiatives are launched, note any seasonal patterns or market changes, and record significant competitor actions.

Set initial benchmarks by starting to measure everything you can, even if it seems basic: time from lead to sale, content usage rates, campaign response rates, and sales team satisfaction with marketing materials. Use these numbers as your starting point. They don't need to be perfect. Document your assumptions by writing down how you think marketing activities impact sales, noting which channels seem to perform better and recording what you believe drives customer decisions. These assumptions will help guide what you measure.

Remember, every company has to start somewhere with data collection. The key is to begin measuring now, even if your initial metrics are rough. You can refine your tracking systems over time, but you can't recover historical data you never collected. Start simple, be consistent, and focus on trends rather than perfect numbers. Within three to six months, you'll have enough data to start making informed decisions and setting realistic improvement goals.

Most importantly, communicate openly with leadership about what you're measuring and why. They'll appreciate your proactive approach to proving marketing's value, even if the initial data isn't as comprehensive as you'd like. Your goal is to show executives the impact that marketing is having on business goals.

LEADING VS. LAGGING INDICATORS

Another excellent metric to begin measuring and discussing with leadership is leading indicators. Many times, I find that companies are only focused on lagging indicators.

Basically, leading indicators are early signals that predict future results, such as an increase in website traffic that may lead to more sales later. In contrast, lagging indicators are measurements of what has already happened, like last quarter's revenue or completed sales.

Leading indicators help you adjust course before results come in, while lagging indicators confirm whether your strategies actually worked.

For clarity, here are some key differences between the two:

Feature	Leading Indicators	Lagging Indicators
Timing	Predicts future outcomes	Measures past outcomes
Focus	Inputs, actions, or early trends	Results or final outcomes

Leading indicators can identify potential issues or opportunities early, while lagging indicators help you evaluate overall success and areas for improvement. Together, they provide a comprehensive performance measurement framework.

If your company is not used to talking about leading indicators, choose a couple that make sense for your business, share them with your peers and leaders, and start measuring them.

HOW TO DETERMINE WHAT METRICS TO TRACK

As a marketing department, your team will get all sorts of jobs and requests from various departments and customers. An easy way to ensure all your projects and initiatives are working toward a key metric is by asking the requester or collaborator what goal the project is trying to meet, then tying your effort and work product to the project as a supporting factor. Here are a few ways you can ask this question:

- "How will success be measured for this specific request or project?" (From this, you can discuss how your input/deliverable will help them get closer to success.)

- "Is this request part of a bigger project or initiative? If so, can you elaborate?"

- "What business impact will this project have?"

- "What business goals or initiatives does this project support?"

- "If this request were not completed at all, what impact would it have on your project or business results?"

List a few leading and lagging indicators that the completion of this project will support. If possible, include examples so the requestor knows what you are looking for.

It's important to determine what impact your team's work is having on overall business goals. For every request you get or every project you are working on, you should think about what metrics to tie them to. Start now: Think about one or two projects that are currently active and narrow down potential metrics for them. If you need additional brainstorming support, apply the tips learned from Step 2: Technology and AI Tools That Actually Help: Open ChatGPT, Claude, or another preferred generative AI tool and enter the following prompt to help you brainstorm:

"You lead a marketing department and need to tie your projects to business goals or revenues. You need to be able to communicate the impact your work has on the business. List out five to seven potential metrics that can be tied to the following project: [Enter project information here]."

If you want a more tailored answer, you can also include this line: "Ask me a few questions so that you can understand my company and industry better and answer to the best of your ability."

HOW TO TELL THE STORY TO EXECUTIVES AND PEERS

Remember the story of Bob the CEO, the one who interrupted a poor engineer's presentation by saying, "I can read faster than you can talk"?

Leaders don't want a data dump; they want a business story supported by data and delivered cohesively.

In order to properly tell the right story, you first need to outline your metrics into three categories:

- Proof of Progress (Are we doing things right?)

  o Milestone metrics

  o Vanity metrics (engagement, impressions, etc.)

- Proof of Impact: Leading Indicators (Are we doing the right things?)

  o Asset adoption rate by sales team

- Customer feedback metrics
- Proof of Value: Lagging Indicators (Are we driving business results?)
  - Sales metrics
  - Lead increases

Once you have the right metrics, you can start putting together your reports to share with leadership. Depending on your business culture, this report can be done in PowerPoint, Word, or another business-approved platform.

After giving an overview of the project(s) and department goals, get right to the storytelling with key metrics that matter to the business. These include (1) leading indicators that prove you are working on the right stuff for future impact (or need to pivot), (2) lagging indicators (like revenue impact), (3) cost efficiencies (if applicable), and (4) market performance (i.e., if you're beating the competition).

Then move on to clear trends, or the interpretation of the metrics. Based on the data, what are you improving or working on? Where is help needed? What tasks are right on track?

Lastly, talk about the next big move: What you are doing based on the data. Discuss any feedback you may be receiving based on this new approach. How are these metrics impacting the type of projects you work on and the priorities you are setting?

I also keep three versions of every report:

1. Executive summary (the outline from above)

2. Department deep dive (full metrics and timelines)

3. Team working doc (all the details)

Leadership gets Version 1, and they can ask for Version 2 if they want more detail. Version 3 stays with the team.

When presenting, I also make sure to say something that is *not* on the slides (thanks for the lesson, Bob) to make sure the leaders are actually listening to me.

The modern approach is to ask AI (ChatGPT, Claude, or ProblemsChatGPT) to help you determine what lagging indicators you can start measuring to show the impact of your team's work on the business. Have ChatGPT ask you questions about your business and the type of work you are doing so that it can answer to the best of its ability. Here is a sample prompt:

"You are the CMO of [company] in [industry], your company is a [local/regional/national/global] player, you sell [service or product] direct to [businesses/consumers], and you need to prepare your marketing metrics for the team and your executive peers. Ask me questions about the industry, the business, and the type of marketing that is done, then outline the lagging indicators I can start measuring and presenting."

Remember, take the time to engage a minimum of three times so that you can get down to the metrics that make sense for you and your business. Then you can take this information, pop it into Beautiful.AI, and have it outline a presentation for your team on the metrics you will be measuring.

Don't worry about being sloppy. Do not overthink it. Just do it, now.

Then take this information and make a list to capture all the data. This will come in handy during review time.

In summary, marketing leaders often struggle to prove the tangible impact of their work on business success. Completing projects on time and within budget is not enough. Executives want to see direct results in revenue, efficiency, and customer acquisition.

Many marketing professionals fall into the trap of tracking every possible metric, creating complex dashboards that fail to answer one fundamental question: "How does this contribute to business growth?" The key to proving marketing's value lies in identifying leading and lagging indicators that align with executive priorities and tying marketing initiatives to measurable business outcomes.

By focusing on metrics that matter, such as marketing-influenced revenue, customer acquisition cost, and sales cycle length, marketing teams can transition from being seen as a cost center to a revenue-driving function. The approach also includes adopting a countdown storytelling method when presenting results to executives, ensuring clarity and impact.

KEY TAKEAWAYS

Marketing work must be tied to business impact. Executives care about revenue, market share, and customer acquisition, not vanity metrics! You can save yourself some time by reducing the data you are tracking. Identify three to five key business-driven metrics, then track those metrics to tie them directly to marketing efforts.

Start talking about leading and lagging indicator metrics. Leading indicators (website traffic, lead generation, etc.) predict success, while lagging indicators (revenue growth, profit margins, etc.) validate it.

Shift from reporting activities to proving impact. Instead of saying, "We increased social media engagement by 50 percent," say, "Our LinkedIn leads are converting 30 percent faster, reducing the sales cycle by fifteen days."

Ask the right questions to tie marketing to business goals. Before executing projects, ask:

- How will success be measured?

- What happens if this initiative is not completed?

- What business problem are we solving?

Structure your reports in a way that clearly tells the story of marketing's impact by first discussing the key metrics that tie the project to the business. Next, discuss major trends, such as where the company is improving and where help is needed. Finally, discuss what marketing is doing next to drive success.

By making these shifts, marketing leaders can prove their worth, gain executive buy-in, and elevate marketing from a support function to a business growth driver.

Tying marketing efforts directly to business impacts, like revenue growth, market share, and profitability, is critical to ensuring marketing has "a seat at the table." The ability to speak the language of executives is what separates marketing leaders from order-takers. Leading conversations with the right focus will ensure you are building credibility and support for you and your team.

FAIL FAST, IMPROVE FASTER

"We need to let you go."

The rest of their words dissolved into white noise; all I could think was, *Don't cry. Don't cry. Don't cry.* I never saw it coming.

I was a director at Rockwell & Sons Manufacturing. My team had expanded and I was now leading two departments. Both were executing well and had a great reputation in the business. Then, after a fifteen-minute meeting on a Thursday afternoon, it was over. The worst part is that my team and I had spent that morning volunteering at a local school, helping clean up their yard and planting flowers. It had been a fun team-building activity. I was feeling grateful for my team and my company for allowing us the time to help in the local community. That afternoon, we all went back to our respective homes to jump into our remote work. Little did I know my work day would last less than two hours.

I cried. Not during the meeting, of course; I held it together until I was able to turn off the camera on my computer. But then I lost it. Seven years of work, gone in fifteen minutes.

The tears came in waves, hot and unstoppable. My chest felt hollow, like someone had scooped out everything inside. I sat there, staring at the black screen where, moments before, emotionless faces had delivered the news with corporate precision. My hands trembled as I reached for my phone, not even sure who to call or what to say. How do you summarize seven years of dedication ending in a 15-minute meeting? The house suddenly felt too quiet, too empty, as if the walls themselves were acknowledging this new absence in my life.

This moment reminded me of something an old mentor once told me: "If you continue down this career path, one day you will be fired, 'laid off,' or 'forced into early retirement.' And you'll have to do the same to others. It's inevitable. A high-rewarding career, in the corporate sense, does not come without risks. Know that it *will* happen. And when it does, you'll remember this conversation."

I remembered nodding when he told me this, thinking I had understood. But I hadn't, not really. There's no preparing for the feelings of shame, betrayal, and fear that wash over you after being let go. A dozen questions instantly flood your mind: *How will I pay my mortgage? What will I tell my family? Who am I without this job title?* The identity I had carefully built over the years suddenly collapsed like a house of cards right before my eyes.

My mentor was right. I had been laid off. And it sucked. It more than sucked; it was devastating. It forced me to confront parts of myself I had conveniently hidden behind meeting schedules and quarterly goals.

That layoff was the first time I was on the receiving end, but I had been part of these types of conversations many times before. My company had been fired as a client by an agency, I'd had to fire people I respected (this one hurts!), and I'd had to lay off good employees and fire poor performers (just like my mentor once said I would).

Each of these experiences taught me something crucial about building resilience. They taught me how to fail with grace and recover stronger. But most importantly, they taught me how to treat others with grace.

I stopped thinking about life in terms of failing or winning. Instead, I started thinking in terms of *learning* or winning.

Remember that agency that fired us as a client? I knew it was coming. I'd had dinner with their president the night before. He was an old colleague, and I could read between the lines. I even bet my boss it would happen, but he'd laughed it off. Sure enough, the next day, they fired us.

My boss was shocked because we were one of their biggest clients. He thought we paid their bills, so we called all the shots. I, however, wasn't shocked at all because I had been in the meetings where tensions were high. I had seen the executive team's displeasure and angst over our working relationship.

The bright side of that agency firing us? It led to a complete restructuring of how we worked with our creative partners. Instead of using one big agency, we built a network of specialized partners. When we did the math a year later, we realized we were getting better work at a 15 percent lower cost.

The biggest lesson from both of these scenarios is about how to fail *the right way*. Here's what each failure taught me:

LESSONS FROM GETTING LAID OFF

Getting laid off is never just about performance. I was delivering results, but I wasn't playing the political game. I wasn't marketing myself internally. I thought my work would speak for itself.

Now I know better: You need to make sure people know the value you're creating. My recovery strategy involved focusing on the metrics that matter to the business (see Step 5: Proving Your Worth), documenting my wins (both big and small), sharing success stories regularly, building relationships across departments, and keeping a "brag file" of achievements based on key metrics (this file is for my personal use and reference). This approach isn't about shameless self-promotion but about ensuring visibility of meaningful contributions that might otherwise go unnoticed. I learned that the most brilliant work means little if decision-makers aren't aware of it.

By thoughtfully communicating my impact and forming genuine connections throughout the organization, I created advocates who understood my value.

LESSONS FROM BEING FIRED

Communication breakdowns rarely happen suddenly. There are always warning signs. We had tense meetings with the agency, where frustrations simmered beneath polite conversation until they blatantly came out as accusations of missed deadlines and project scope creep. Expectations were unclear, leaving both sides assuming different priorities, and frustrated teams began avoiding and blaming each other instead of collaborating.

Instead of addressing these issues head-on, we kept pushing forward, hoping things would improve on their own. They didn't. The relationship deteriorated slowly, like storm clouds gathering for hours before the downpour finally began. In retrospect, we should have called for a reset meeting at the first signs of trouble to clarify deliverables and responsibilities. We should have had the courage to address the underlying issues rather than just the symptoms.

By the time we received our termination notice, it felt both shocking and inevitable. The business relationship had died months ago; the paperwork was only a formality.

This is the recovery strategy that I now employ:

- Regular relationship check-ins

- Clear communication protocols

- Early problem intervention

- Mutual success metrics

LESSONS FROM CONSUMER BEHAVIOR

Sometimes the biggest mistake is waiting too long to find out if something is working. Moving fast and learning as you go beats planning perfectly before starting every time. Here are some examples of businesses that did not wait:

Today, you know Instagram as a photo-sharing app, but it actually started as Burbn, a check-in app like Foursquare. The developers noticed that users weren't checking in much, but they were sharing tons of photos. They could have spent months trying to "fix" the check-in features, but instead, they completely pivoted based on real user behavior.

Slack started as an internal communication tool for a game called Glitch that ultimately failed. The chat tool was built for internal use, but the developers noticed this "side project" was solving a bigger problem. Today, the Slack app is used in offices all over the world, and the company behind it is worth billions.

Human behavior isn't always predictable, so it's important to learn and get feedback from actual customers. This real feedback is worth much more than any starting theories and expectations, as we've learned from Instagram and Slack.

According to behavioral economics, humans often make irrational decisions due to biases, emotions, social influences, and cognitive limitations, and these decisions deviate (sometimes completely) from theoretical economics. In other words, our assumptions are often wrong. Because of this, I recommend you launch early to gather feedback that can be pivotal for success.

Just launch. I know this is easier said than done; humans are hardwired to avoid failure. Consider this example of a marketing campaign for a subscription service:

A streaming service is trying to encourage customers to subscribe to their premium plan. They run two versions of a campaign, each with the same financial outcome, but framed differently:

Version 1: Framed as a loss

- "You're losing $20 a month in benefits by not upgrading to Premium."

Version 2: Framed as a gain

- "Upgrade to Premium and gain $20 a month in additional value!"

Time and again, studies have shown that the first version, the one framed as a loss, outperforms the second. This is because humans feel losses much more strongly than gains.

People are irrationally driven to avoid losses, so the idea of "losing" $20 a month creates a stronger emotional reaction than "gaining" the same amount. Behavioral economics calls this phenomenon "loss aversion:" On average, humans value avoiding losses about twice as much as acquiring equivalent gains. This explains why we naturally avoid failure or loss, but waiting to perfect something before launching will usually cost you in the long run.

A tactic I use to continue making progress without getting caught in the trap of "perfection pending" is what I call "first draft courage:" the willingness to send out something that's "good enough" in order to get feedback on it. This is also known as the 40/80 rule, and it's changed everything about how my team and I work. The idea is to get a project to 40 percent perfect, then ship it for feedback. Based on that feedback, improve the final product to 80 percent perfect through structured revisions, then deliver it. As for that final 20 percent? Only if the ROI justifies it.

In practice, we use this rule all the time. Just recently, we had a major client report due. The traditional approach would have been to spend three days getting it as close to perfect as possible by reviewing it internally multiple times, polishing every detail before sending it to the client. Instead, we spent three hours on a solid first draft (40 percent), sent it to the client for initial feedback, refined based on their input (to 80 percent), and only perfected the elements they truly cared about. The result? We got client input three days earlier, identified issues we hadn't considered, saved about fifteen hours of work, and delivered a better final product.

This is not about sending sloppy work, nor is it about sending a rough draft as a final product. It's about sending work that's ready for input. The key is having a structured iteration process so that you can get the right feedback without losing momentum.

When using this approach, make sure to first set the right expectations with your stakeholders. Make it clear that this version is for initial review and is not the final product. I typically say, "Let me give you something to react to." This will set the right expectations and ensure that the team and your stakeholders are in the right mindset when reviewing and providing feedback. You will also want to communicate the timeline and the benefit of having them "react" to an earlier version so that the team and the project can move faster than a traditional timeline.

With this in mind, expect feedback that will lead to an average of two rounds of edits. Knowing this in advance will allow you to work this time into your timeline and not let it wound your pride. Your final product will be better for it.

Also be sure to ask for specific feedback. A good example is this book. I sent a rough draft to three beta readers and asked them two questions: (1) "Are there any confusing parts or sections?" and (2) "What do you like?" This allowed me to keep the feedback within reason and make the necessary edits and improvements.

This approach works because it allows teams to work in parallel streams, issues to surface earlier, and projects to maintain momentum. The cost of delay (those three days of perfecting) usually exceeds the benefit of perfection, especially when early feedback might change everything anyway. And honestly, we know that most people will have an opinion on the work or the output of marketing, so gathering that feedback early can save you a lot of time in the long run.

Again, keep in mind that this does not give you permission to send half-baked work. Your 40 percent should be

- strategically sound,

- professionally presented,

- clearly marked as the initial draft, and

- ready for meaningful feedback.

Think of it like serving a meal: 40 percent is the taste test, 80 percent is the meal, and the last 20 percent is the fancy plating that only a few people will care about. The key is knowing your audience and what level of polish they actually need versus what you think they want.

THE GAP BETWEEN PERFECTION AND PROGRESS

In the pursuit of perfection, we often forget that progress itself creates value. Remember these key principles:

- A 40 percent solution delivered today beats a perfect solution delivered too late.

- Quick failures are simply early warnings of what needs to change.

- The cost of delay often exceeds the cost of imperfection.

The next time your team hesitates to release that first draft or launch that pilot program, ask them, "What will cost more: the time we'll spend trying to make this perfect, or the insights we'll miss by not getting it in front of our audience today?"

Build your buffers, embrace calculated risks, and remember that the fastest path to excellence isn't a straight line but a series of well-planned iterations and improvements.

Failure is never comfortable, but it's inevitable. Learn how to pivot quickly, extract insights from failures, and apply those lessons in real time. This is what separates resilient marketing leaders from those who get stuck repeating the same cycles and never doing anything truly remarkable.

KEY TAKEAWAYS

Everyone will face a career setback. This is a fact. What matters is what you do next. Getting laid off, losing clients, or making bad hires are all part of the leadership journey. Treat these failures as learning experiences. This mental shift will help you embrace the inevitable and grow from the experience.

Learning from real-world behavior is far more valuable than waiting for the "perfect plan." Adopt a first-draft mentality: "Let me give you something to react to." People respond better to something tangible than to a blank page. The key is not to avoid failure but to fail the right way, by learning quickly, pivoting effectively, and treating others with grace. Rethink failure to put yourself and your team in the driver's seat.

Use the 40/80 rule to stop waiting for perfection and start gathering real feedback. At 40 percent complete, send for feedback; at 80 percent complete, iterate and refine; and only aim for 100 percent complete if necessary. This prevents delays, ensures real-time adjustments, and improves efficiency.

This brings us to the final critical piece of the puzzle: your team.

Assembling a high-performing marketing team isn't just about hiring talented people. It's about ensuring they're in the right roles, aligned with the company's goals, and operating at their highest potential. The right team is well-positioned and structured for growth. This is not easy. You'll hire great people who turn out to be the wrong fit. You'll have to make tough calls about performance. And you'll realize that sometimes, it's not the individual who's failing; it's the role that wasn't designed correctly.

THE RIGHT PEOPLE, THE RIGHT SEATS (INSPIRED BY JIM COLLINS' CONCEPT IN "GOOD TO GREAT")

"The moment you feel the need to tightly manage someone, you've made a hiring mistake."[5] —James C. Collins, *Good to Great: Why Some Companies Make the Leap... And Others Don't*

From AI that multiplies your productivity to freelancers who add specialized expertise, we've covered the tools and resources you can leverage to build a scalable marketing team. But all the tools and resources in the world won't matter if you have the wrong people on your team. You need the right team in place in order to truly build a scalable marketing team.

---

[5] Jim Collins, *Good to Great: Why Some Companies Make the Leap... And Others Don't (Good to Great, 1)*, (New York: Harper Business, 2001).

Think about that dispatch system I mentioned at the beginning of the book, the one handling 36,000 trucks a month. The technology and processes were crucial, but what really made it work were the four people running it. Each person brought something essential: Julia had tenacity, Gary was reliable, Tom had experience, and the bonus dispatcher gave extra support. The system worked because we had the right people in the right roles.

But building and maintaining a high-performing team isn't always comfortable. Sometimes, despite our best efforts at hiring and training, we discover that someone just isn't the right fit. Maybe they're in the wrong role, or maybe they're on the wrong team entirely. As a marketing leader focused on building a scalable team and getting your seat at the table, you need to be prepared for these situations.

Jim Collins puts it perfectly in *Good to Great*: "… I know this much: If we get the right people on the bus, the right people in the right seats, and the wrong people off the bus, then we'll figure out how to take it someplace great. … [If] you have the wrong people, it doesn't matter whether you discover the right direction; you still won't have a great company."[6]

Let's dig into what he means:

---

[6]   Collins, *Good to Great (1)*.

- **The wrong people on the bus**: Employees who are not a good fit for the company, possibly because of a misalignment of culture or values

- **The right people**: Employees who share the company's values and are committed to the organization's success and are loyal to the company

- **The right seats**: Employees who are operating in their area of greatest skill and passion

Why is this important? When the right people are in the right seats, the organization can focus on a shared vision and work toward common goals. You won't have to worry too much about motivating them and questioning their work quality.

To build a team with all the right people in the right seats, you'll need to start with the most uncomfortable step: getting the wrong people off the bus.

THE WRONG PEOPLE ON THE BUS

In your long career as a marketing leader, you will reach a point where you need to separate someone from the company. If this separation is due to poor performance, you will likely use a traditional performance improvement plan (PIP).

This is when someone is fired with cause, mainly for not performing to the level the job requires. Letting someone go because of a PIP is a long and detailed process. Your human resources department likely has a standard procedure you need to follow, which may look something like this:

1. As the manager, you are required to give the employee feedback on work performance and expectations and to supply the appropriate tools to properly complete the work. A formal review with the employee about not meeting expectations is also required.

2. Depending on the company's policy, you may need to write a warning to the employee and record all conversations about their work performance.

3. If the performance does not improve after a designated period of time, you will formally file the PIP. This will include specific goals or tasks the employee needs to accomplish at the expected level and by the agreed-upon date.

The idea behind a PIP is to help an employee rise to their expected level of performance before they face the last resort of being fired. To be honest, though, rarely have I seen this work out. The only people I ever witnessed "survive" a PIP were later fired by their next leader. This just tells me the original manager didn't properly manage the employee. It's sad, but carrying a poor performer is not worth the effort. You risk lowering the team's overall performance, and the team may start to lose respect for you.

In one vivid memory, I had to let go of a young digital marketing employee who was well-liked by all. He was personable, had good ideas, and was an overall joy. But he was also very absent, literally. On any given week, he would miss a couple of days of work. He called in sick, he ran into car troubles, he had to take his dog to the vet, and he suffered a death in the family (and another one). The absenteeism became too much, and some projects were greatly impacted by his absence. I had no choice but to let him go.

Funnily enough, the next day, one of my team members came up to me and said, "Finally, someone fired that guy! He was nice, but man, was he tough to work with! We couldn't count on him for anything; he'd randomly not show up for work and leave us all holding the bag. It's about time he got canned."

When you have low performers and unreliable employees, others will notice. The saying "One bad apple spoils the bunch" is true. Employees who are not a good fit need to be dealt with, whether with extra training, reassignment of work, or, worst-case scenario, a PIP plan.

CULTURAL FIT

Remember the story about Sarah, the contractor who was perfect on paper but a nightmare in practice? That experience, along with other similar ones, taught me the importance of cultural fit. Sarah had all the right technical skills, but her approach did not mesh with our company. In short, she was on the wrong bus.

As you continue to build capacity within your team, you will inevitably encounter people who are on the wrong bus. Keeping them on your team will only cause inefficiencies, frustration, and misalignment that will slow down your team's efforts. It may be uncomfortable, but you need to get them off the bus—better sooner than later.

I've been on both sides of this equation: I've had to let people go, and I've been let go myself. Neither is easy. But if you're serious about building a scalable marketing team that delivers consistent results, you need to get comfortable with making tough personnel decisions. Work with your HR team to ensure you are being fair and honest about your employees' output and their alignment with the company.

THE RIGHT PEOPLE IN THE RIGHT SEATS

Once you've taken the wrong people off the bus, you should be left with the right people: employees who share the company's values and who are committed to the organization's success. These are the people who don't need to be tightly managed, to have their work double-checked, or to be questioned about their level of motivation and commitment. These are the people you need on your team, who will improve your team's scalability.

Your next focus is ensuring that you have the right people in the right seats: employees in roles that match their skills and the organization's needs (i.e., roles that allow each employee to operate in their "genius zone").

Let me share a story about getting this wrong before getting it right. We had an amazing designer—creative and technically skilled with a great eye for detail. We promoted her to creative director because … well, that's what you do with great designers, right?

Fast-forward six months: She was miserable! The team was struggling, projects were delayed, and quality was suffering. The problem? We'd taken someone brilliant at execution and put them in a role that required entirely different skills. We were losing a great designer and gaining a frustrated manager. The fix? We created a new role: senior creative specialist. It offered the same pay as a creative director role, but now she could focus on doing the work she loved and mentoring others, not managing processes and budgets.

In the end, she returned to doing what she was good at, the team got their mentor back, quality improved, and everyone was happier.

At a different company, I was taking over a marketing department, and one particular person, a creative designer named Jessica, was clearly in the wrong seat. She seemed frustrated and unhappy with her work. Her prior manager told me that she was difficult to work with and that she would take every criticism or offer for coaching as a direct insult. Once I met with Jessica myself, however, it quickly became clear to me that she passionately cared about doing a good job. She was vested in the company's long-term success and would even work late hours to do the best job possible.

The real problem, as it turned out, was that she had been outgrown by other designers. As our company evolved, we increased our standards and started hiring designers with broader experience and edgier designs. Jessica, meanwhile, was falling behind the curve.

One thing I did notice was that Jessica would quickly volunteer for any web work and go out of her way to learn more about digital marketing. She was also very interested in improving the department's digital asset management system in hopes of improving the team's overall productivity. As I continued to work with Jessica, I realized she was in the wrong seat. She had outgrown her role as a creative designer, and the company had evolved to need a different level of designer.

At this time, I was leading the project management team and MARTECH (marketing technology). We moved Jessica to the role of a MARTECH coordinator, and the outcome was phenomenal! Jessica embraced her role and even got a few more certifications to improve her skills on some of our platforms. She overhauled our DAM, which led to an improvement in our designers' efficiency and turnaround times. She became our marketing automation lead and helped lead many successful campaigns. Finally, Jessica was happy, and the business was better for it. She was now in the right seat.

As a leader, your responsibility is to ensure that each person on your team is in the right seat, contributing in a way that aligns with their skills, their passions, and your company's needs. When you get this right, your marketing engine runs efficiently, delivering results with less friction. To do this well, you must first be clear about the key positions your organization needs. This includes determining whether each role should be in-house or outsourced, identifying specific skill sets required, and defining the appropriate level of expertise for success in each position (see Steps 3 and 4 in this book).

Inevitably, as a leader, you'll encounter situations where someone is not the right fit for their seat. When this happens, make sure you have confirmed they are the right person (like Jessica). If they are, you may need to restructure your team, adjust the reporting structure, or reassign a role to better align with the organization's direction and the employee's strengths.

A strong, scalable team will evolve as the organization grows, and sometimes, that means making difficult but necessary changes.

KEY TAKEAWAYS

A scalable marketing team requires the right people in the right seats.

The "right people" are the employees who share your company's values and are committed to success. The "right seats" are the roles that are best suited to said employees' greatest strengths and passions. This allows for appropriate alignment and effort toward the company's success. If alignment is off, inefficiencies, frustration, and poor performance follow.

How to ensure the right fit:

- Clearly define key roles and skill sets needed for success.

- Be willing to adjust roles and restructure when necessary.

- Proactively address misalignment—don't let poor fits linger.

In your long and successful career, you will eventually come across misalignment. If you know you have the wrong person on the bus (an employee who lacks necessary skills or values), they need to be taken off the bus (gracefully!). Here are a few tips for how to handle these situations:

- Use a performance improvement plan (PIP) when an employee isn't meeting expectations.

- If restructuring a role, be honest and fair—some employees simply outgrow the company's needs.

- Avoid carrying dead weight—low performers bring down team morale and productivity.

Right person in the wrong seat? If someone has potential but is in the wrong role, adjust their position or support them in their skill training or development. This can also mean restructuring. Sometimes the business evolves and roles change, even for good performers, so it's up to you to help your people find the right seats.

The last key takeaway is to hire for growth. This can be achieved by favoring adaptability over years of experience, a growth mindset over fixed skills, and cultural fit over technical perfection.

All of this effort may seem overwhelming, but it's so worth it. Once you have all the right people in the right seats, your bus will be ready to drive off toward success!

CONCLUSION

Although marketing is exciting, I hate to admit that early in my career, I was a bit embarrassed to be part of the "marketing department." I did not fit the mold of a traditional marketer (I'm not a creative designer), and I feared I would not be taken seriously as a businesswoman, so I would come up with excuses for my career choice when asked about my work.

By now, I hope that when asked, "So, what do you do?" your answer will be a confident, "I build and operate business growth engines through marketing."

Because that's also what marketing is all about.

You will quickly disarm people, and it'll surely be a conversation starter. One that you can tackle with excitement by stating the metrics from your recent projects, whether that's a 10 percent increase in sales through your partnership on a recent campaign or a 15 percent decrease in retrieval time because of your DAM implementation.

After reading this book, I hope you now realize the size of your team or budget doesn't determine your success. What matters is how you build and operate your marketing team.

Throughout this book, we've explored how to structure and scale your marketing team. Whether you're a solo marketer or leading a large team, the principles remain the same: Prioritize ruthlessly, fix the leaks (processes) first, leverage technology, scale wisely by using allies and traditional resources, prove your worth, fail faster but improve faster and ensure the right people are in the right seats.

Remember, these tools are most effective when they work together as a system. Just like my dispatch team from way back when, your marketing operation will thrive when people, processes, and tools are aligned.

You don't need to implement everything at once. Start where you're feeling the most pressure:

- Drowning in manual tasks? Start with automation.

- Struggling to prove your team's value? Focus on the metrics that tell your story.

- Lacking specialized skills? Build your internal and external resource network.

- Constantly fighting fires? Establish basic workflows and ruthlessly prioritize what matters most.

The marketing engine you build today creates momentum for tomorrow. These systems, tools, and mindsets help shift marketing from a reactive cost center to a proactive growth driver. As your systems scale, your influence grows. And with that influence, you earn a seat at the table.

New technologies will emerge, channels will shift, and business needs will evolve. But the foundational principles we've covered will remain constant:

- Limit your project list to only the top five (prioritize ruthlessly).

- Never stop improving, by first fixing the leaks

- Balance technology with human insight.

- Build support resources that can scale.

- Prove your worth by starting with business impact.

- Move fast and learn faster.

- Ensure you have they right people in the right roles.

You've got the tools. You know how to use them. Now it's time to dig in!

For additional resources, templates, and worksheets, visit https://bit.ly/DiggPlaybook.

Want to accelerate your progress and outsource some high-impact projects? Learn how we can work together at www.thediggagency.com!

I look forward to *digging in* with you and helping you build a scalable team, prove your value, and earn your seat at the table—where you belong!

ACKNOWLEDGMENTS

They say it takes a village to raise a child. As it turns out, it also takes one to write a book. This work wouldn't exist without the support, guidance, and encouragement of many people.

First and foremost, to my husband: Your unwavering support made this book possible. Thank you for creating space in our busy lives for me to write, and for believing in this project even when I doubted it. Those extra hours you spent with our boys so I could write "just one more section" meant everything.

To my parents for always encouraging me, even when the details of my "projects" were a bit unclear. To my sisters for immediately signing up to read the book, even if the content is not applicable to you. Now that's support. And to my kiddos for showing support in the glimmer in your eye whenever you talked about how "Mom is writing a book."

To the many colleagues and leaders I've worked with throughout my career—the good, the bad, and even the challenging—thank you. Each of you taught me something valuable about marketing, leadership, and myself. Your collective influence shapes these pages in ways both subtle and profound. An extra big shout-out to Angie Marcelli, who gave me a chance in marketing, and Jim Hand, who gave me the opportunity to lead in logistics when I had minimal experience.

Special thanks to Tricia Mirchandani at T Collective, whose thoughtful feedback helped sharpen these ideas into their clearest form. Your insights were invaluable in bringing this book to life.

The team at Self-Publishing, particularly Ali and Kurt, provided the guidance and structure needed to transform this from an idea into reality. Thank you for showing me the path forward and keeping me on it.

To the talented editors at Wandering Words: Thank you for helping polish these words until they shone, while ensuring my voice remained authentic throughout.

And to my beta readers, who generously gave their time to provide feedback on early drafts: Your perspectives helped make this book more valuable and actionable for everyone who reads it.

Writing this book has been a journey of reflection, growth, and sharing. To everyone who played a part, whether mentioned here or not: thank you. This book exists because of you.

APPENDIX: TEMPLATES AND CHEAT SHEETS

Throughout this book, we've covered a lot of ground—from leveraging AI to managing freelancers, from building internal alliances to measuring business impact. Now it's time to put it all in one place. Think of this section as your quick-reference guide for building a scalable team and earning your seat at the table.

I've designed this section to be practical and actionable. You'll find templates, checklists, and frameworks organized by category. Whether you're about to hire your first freelancer, implement a new AI tool, or justify your marketing impact to leadership, you can flip to this section and find exactly what you need.

Here you can find a mix of

- key tools and resources

- templates and frameworks

- implementation tips

I encourage you to bookmark this section, add your own notes, and adapt these tools to your specific situation. After all, that's what building a marketing engine is all about: taking proven approaches and making them work for your unique circumstances.

Let's dig into your marketing operations toolkit!

(Note: Many of these resources and platforms are continuously evolving and changing. Please visit https://bit.ly/DiggPlaybook for the most recent information and recommendations.)

HOW DO YOU EAT AN ELEPHANT: TASK PRIORITIZATION FRAMEWORK

Regardless of your marketing budget or team size, you will always have more on your to-do list than you have time. There will always be things to fix, new initiatives to try, and bigger goals to go after. Therefore, before you can build a high-performing marketing engine, scale your operations, and earn your executive seat, you must first master the art of prioritization. Doing good work will often depend on first deciding what the right work is. Plainly said, you need to prioritize what you will work on and what you will not work on. You need to narrow down your priority list to only the top five projects.

The first step is to work on aligning your projects to the business goals and objectives. From here, you can use three different frameworks to help you narrow down to the priorities that truly matter to the business. There is the Impact vs. Explosion assessment (one of my favorites), the Impact vs. Effort Matrix, and the Eisenhower Matrix. Each is explained below:

IMPACT VS. EXPLOSION ASSESSMENT

This isn't some complex scoring system. It's about asking practical questions to help you boil down to what truly is breaking (will explode) and prioritizing that work over what can be categorized as a nice-to-have.

Here are some starter questions to help you figure out if what you think you should be working on truly matters:

- What will break if we do not do this at all? (explode)

- What's actually breaking right now? (explode)

- What will happen if we do this well? (impact)

- What needs a longer-term solution? (impact)

Compare projects through this approach, then prioritize what's "breaking" (i.e., what will explode).

IMPACT VS. EFFORT MATRIX

The Impact vs. Effort Matrix helps evaluate tasks based on two key dimensions: the potential impact of completing the task and the effort required to do so. This creates four quadrants:

- Quick Wins (high impact, low effort) – Tasks that provide significant value while requiring minimal resources. These should be your first priority, as they offer the best return on investment.

- Big Projects (high impact, high effort) – Tasks that deliver substantial value but require significant resources. These warrant careful planning and dedicated time blocks for execution.

- Fill-Ins (low impact, low effort) – Tasks that are easy to complete but offer minimal value. Handle these during downtime or delegate when possible.

- Thankless Tasks (low impact, high effort) – Tasks that consume significant resources while providing minimal value. Consider eliminating, automating, or redesigning these processes.

The impact/effort matrix

A simple approach to prioritizing work.

Quick wins
High impact,
and low effort

Big projects
High impact,
but high effort

LOW EFFORT   **HIGH EFFORT**

HIGH IMPACT

LOW IMPACT

Fill-in jobs
Low effort,
low impact

Thankless tasks
Low impact,
AND high effort

Source: BiteSize Learning

EISENHOWER MATRIX

Named after President Dwight D. Eisenhower, this framework categorizes tasks based on urgency and importance.

Important and urgent tasks require immediate attention and have significant consequences. Examples include crisis management, pressing deadlines, and time-sensitive problems. These should be prioritized.

Important but not urgent tasks contribute to long-term goals and strategic objectives. These include planning, relationship building, and personal development. Schedule these tasks before they become urgent and plan out resources for them.

Not important but urgent tasks demand attention but don't contribute significantly to your goals. Often these are interruptions or requests from others. Consider delegating these tasks when possible or delaying the delivery time.

Not important and not urgent tasks neither contribute to your goals nor require immediate attention. These might include excessive social media use or unnecessary meetings. Eliminate these tasks if possible.

Eisenhower Matrix

A matrix used to help with productivity.

	URGENT	**NOT URGENT**
IMPORTANT	**DO** Do it now! URGENT AND IMPORTANT	**SCHEDULE** Schedule for later IMPORTANT BUT NOT URGENT
NOT IMPORTANT	**DELEGATE** NOT IMPORTANT BUT URGENT	**ELIMINATE** NOT IMPORTANT AND NOT URGENT

FIX THE LEAKS FIRST (FROM STEP 1)

Kaizen is Japanese for "improvement" or "change for the better."This methodology emphasizes that improvement is an ongoing journey rather than a destination. The power of Kaizen and its foundational principle is to focus on making small, incremental improvements consistently over time, rather than seeking perfect solutions immediately.

Implementation begins by documenting current processes in detail. Analyze the present state carefully, then develop targeted improvement plans. Implementation focuses on manageable changes that can be readily adopted and measured. Review what works and what doesn't, then adjust accordingly. This creates a cycle of continuous refinement and improvement.

The 1 percent rule is a key concept in Kaizen. It's the power of small improvements compounded over time. By targeting just a 1 percent improvement each day, organizations can achieve significant transformation over thirty, sixty, or ninety days. As part of the Kaizen approach, you can apply the 5 Whys analysis to help analyze a current problem and fix it.

THE 5 WHYS ANALYSIS

The 5 Whys is an iterative problem-solving technique that helps identify the root cause of an issue by repeatedly asking "Why?" until you reach the fundamental source. Here's how it works:

1. Start with the initial problem statement. This should be a specific statement that describes the issue you're investigating.

2. Next, ask why the problem occurs and determine a fact-based answer. This reveals the first level of causation.

3. Continue to ask "Why?" for each answer, diving deeper into causation. Each response should be based on facts and direct observation rather than assumptions.

Usually by the fifth "Why," you'll uncover the root cause. Sometimes you'll need fewer or more questions, but five serves as a helpful baseline.

Once you identify the root cause, develop countermeasures that address the fundamental issue rather than just treating the symptoms.

FISHBONE (ISHIKAWA) DIAGRAM

Another approach to determine the root cause of issues and improve a given process is the Fishbone Diagram. This is also known as the Cause and Effect or Ishikawa Diagram. It resembles a fish skeleton, with the problem stated at the head and potential causes arranged along the bones.

Similar to the 5 Whys approach, start by clearly defining the problem, then brainstorm potential causes within each category. Continue breaking down causes into more specific factors until you identify actionable items.

Standard categories include people, process, equipment, materials, environment, and management, though these can be customized to your specific context.

- Primary Causes – These are major potential causes within each category, represented as large bones connecting to the spine.

- Secondary Causes – These are detailed factors contributing to the primary causes, shown as smaller bones branching off from the primary ones.

Once you've identified the root causes, prioritize them based on impact and develop targeted solutions for the most significant factors.

Fishbone (Ishikawa) Diagram

A brainstorming tool using categories to explore root cause.

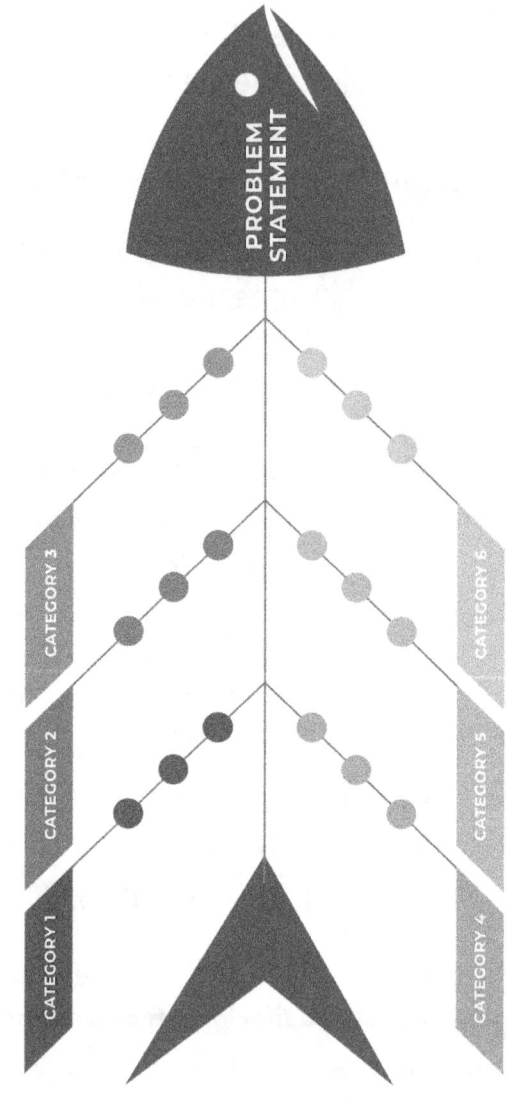

THE IN-HOUSE VS. OUTSOURCE FORMULA (FROM STEP 3)

When determining which marketing functions to outsource, consider the strategic importance of the role to your long-term marketing strategy. Tasks that are central to your core business might be better kept in-house, while non-core functions could be candidates for outsourcing.

Evaluate how frequently the work is needed. Functions that require consistent attention may justify a full-time hire, whereas occasional needs might be more efficiently handled by external specialists who can be engaged as required.

Assess your team's internal expertise. If your current staff lacks certain specialized skills, outsourcing to experts can fill these gaps without investing in training or developing those capabilities internally.

Finally, analyze cost efficiency. Compare the total expenses of hiring, training, and maintaining an employee against the costs of working with external partners. Outsourcing often eliminates overhead costs like benefits, office space, and equipment, potentially offering significant savings for certain functions.

Score each of the following categories on a 1–5 scoring scale (1 low, 5 high):

Capabilities Scoring for [enter job title here]		
Category	[Job title] details	Scoring 1-5
Strategic Importance	A Higher impact on long-term marketing strategy= higher score	
Frequency of Need	High frequency = higher score	
Internal Expertise	High internal alignment with skills = higher score	
Cost Efficiency	In-house hiring is more cost-effective than outsourcing = higher score	
	Total Points	

Once you are done, add up the scores to determine what approach is best to scale your team:

- 16–20 points: In-house

- 11–15 points: Hybrid approach

- 0–10 points: Outsource

BEYOND THE ORG CHART: HOW TO SCALE WITH INTERNAL ALLIES AND EXTERNAL EXPERTS (FROM STEP 4)

LEVERAGING INTERNAL RESOURCES (CROSS-DEPARTMENT SUPPORT)

Leveraging internal resources outside of marketing may require HR support, mainly because of various labor laws. Therefore, I recommend you approach your HR leader and ask them to establish a formal rotational program.

This might slow down the process if you need some immediate help, because you'll need to outline the approach, edit it, and have the HR lead review it before implementing it.

However, you can try to speed up the process by outlining the program and limiting your request to a trial run. Narrow down the departments or positions that can be part of this trial program, and the HR team may be more lenient with their approval.

If you do *not* have a formal HR program, you can approach a senior VP, the president, or a department leader for support in this approach.

Below is a short template you can use for reference:

PROGRAM OUTLINE:

- Program duration and expectations
- Learning objectives
- Eligible individuals and how they will be selected for the program
- Additional program features:
  a. Mentorship components
  b. Evaluation criteria

PROJECT SCOPE

1. Overview:
   - Department:
   - Project Title:
   - Project Sponsor: [Name of person who will "supervise" the individual]
   - Duration: [Start Date – End Date]

- Executive Summary: [A brief overview explaining the project's purpose, goals, and expected impact]

2. Project Objectives
   - Primary Goal:
   - Success Metrics: [Specific, measurable outcomes]
   - Business Value: [Expected benefits and ROI]

3. Scope
   - In Scope: [What will be delivered]
   - Out of Scope: [What is explicitly excluded]
   - Constraints: [Time, budget, and resource limitations]

4. Project Team (support)
   - Core Team Members and Roles:
   - Stakeholders:
   - External Partners/Vendors:

5. Timeline and Milestones:

6. Budget *(if applicable)*:

7. Project Closure
   - Handover Requirements:
   - Documentation Needs:

- O Success Evaluation:

- O Lessons Learned:

SELECTING THE RIGHT AGENCY

Agencies will always serve a critical role in your scalable team. Choosing the right agency should be based on criteria that are relevant to the project and your organization. I recommend creating a standardized scorecard to use when evaluating agencies. Below is a typical scorecard I use that helps me, and other key stakeholders, rate an agency across similar factors:

	Agency 1	Agency 2	Agency 3	Agency 4
Cost (Do not rate this, just enter a $ amount)	$XX,XXX	$XX,XXX	$XX,XXX	$XX,XXX
Value for Investment				
Cultural Fit				
Industry Experience				
CAPABILITIES 1				
Capabilities 2				
Capabilities 3				
System & Software Alignment				
Total Scoring				
Scoring	1 – Very low 2 – Low 3 – Average 4 – High 5 – Very High			

AGENCY ONBOARDING AND KICKOFF

The first sixty days of any agency relationship are crucial. This is when you set the foundation for success or plant the seeds of failure. Below is an approach that has worked well for me in the past:

Week 1: Onboarding

- Complete all administrative requirements (NDAs, security access, etc.).

    o Schedule team introductions.

- Share brand guidelines and key documentation.

- Set up communication channels and tools.

- Establish regular meeting cadence (I recommend weekly status meetings and bi-weekly check-ins with the account executives).

First forty-five days: Focus on alignment

- Weekly status meetings with the core team

- Bi-weekly check-ins with account executives

- Implementation of the project dashboard

- First milestone review

- Process adjustment as needed

In order to maintain a healthy agency relationship, I recommend using a structured approach for check-in meetings and reports. Below is a checklist of items that can be included in your dashboards and check-in meetings:

1. Weekly dashboard updates

    - Project status and milestone tracking

    - Budget utilization

    - Upcoming deliverables

    - Risks and issues

    - Resource allocation

2. Bi-weekly check-ins with account executives

    - Scope review

    - Relationship health check

    - Strategic alignment discussion

    - Forward-looking planning

The last component I recommend is performance reviews. Depending on the duration of your project, you can do these quarterly or biannually. The purpose of these reviews is to ensure a healthy and productive relationship with your agency. During performance reviews, you will rate each other on points like punctuality, quality of execution, communication, and scope adherence.

Performance reviews can become quite sophisticated, with scaling rates and formal surveys, but I recommend keeping yours as simple as possible. Below is a simple template you can use for your reviews:

Agency Performance Review						
Agency Name						
Project Title(s)						
Date						
Category	Must Improve	Fair	Good	Very Good	Excellent	Why did you select this score?
Account Management				X		
Budget & Financials		X				
Project Management Skills			X			
Scope Adherence		X				
On-Time Execution			X			
Quality of Execution			X			
Response Time				X		
Overall Communication					X	
Team Support				X		

Agency Performance Review						
Team Availability					X	
[Other category relevant to your company]				X		
Total Scoring		2	3	4	2	
Qualitative Comments						
Suggested Improvements						

BUILDING YOUR FREELANCE DREAM TEAM

Here's my proven process for finding and keeping great freelancers:

1. The Testing Phase

   - Start with a small project.

   - Set clear success metrics.

   - Evaluate both work quality and team fit.

   - Get feedback from key stakeholders.

2. The Integration Process

- Ensure proper onboarding (even for short-term freelancers).

- Set up clear communication channels.

- Define escalation paths.

- Conduct regular check-ins.

3. The Long Game

- Keep in touch between projects.

- Share upcoming opportunities early.

- Provide constructive feedback.

- Treat them like **valued partners**, not vendors.

PRO TIPS FOR FREELANCE SUCCESS

1. Clear Contracts

- Spell out deliverables in detail.

- Define revision limits.

- Set clear payment terms.

- Include confidentiality clauses.

2. Setting Boundaries Early

- Working hours and availability

- Communication preferences

- Decision-making authority

- Project scope limits

3. Creating a Feedback Loop

    - Regular check-ins

        ○ Weekly fifteen-minute check-ins may suffice for smaller basic projects.

    - Two-way feedback sessions

    - End-of-project reviews

    - Improvement discussions

HOW TO FIND FREELANCERS AND CONTRACTORS

Thanks to modern technology, finding and hiring freelancers and contractors has never been easier! The challenge now lies in identifying, vetting, and managing freelance resources. Below is a list of resources you can use to find freelancers and contractors:

Online Platforms: These are good for when you have a project with very specific deliverables. Many times, communication with freelancers on these platforms will be limited to emails and text chats, so make sure your project can be easily written out and defined with samples to ensure you get the outcome you need. I've used these platforms to find freelancers for designs (like iconography), templates for sell sheets, and Excel dashboards:

- Upwork

- 99designs (for creatives only)

- Fiverr Pro

- Working Not Working (for creatives only)

There are also staffing companies you can use; throughout the years, I've relied on Kforce, a local and very effective staffing agency. You can also reach out to local industry network groups like chambers of commerce and the American Marketing Association.

Another avenue to find freelancers and contractors is your professional network. Chances are good that your network will know someone who may be qualified for your project. Your professional network includes current and former colleagues, school alumni, industry peers, agencies, and LinkedIn connections.

When hiring a freelancer, be sure to put out a detailed project brief. For templates, check out https://bit.ly/DiggPlaybook.

WHEN AND HOW TO HIRE AN INTERN

Interns can be an excellent resource to help you scale your team. Interns are good for projects that do not require extensive skill sets and experience. One way to determine if your team can benefit from an intern is by evaluating your team's workload:

- Are you or your team spending significant time (five or more hours a week) on routine tasks?

- Do you have a backlog of data entry or research projects?

- Do you have a long list of content needs that are not being met?

- Do you have seasonal spikes when you could use more help (trade shows, events, campaigns, launches, etc.)?

I've used interns for various menial tasks, such as research data collection and basic analysis. In the digital realm, you can use an intern to gather social media metrics, research customer trends, and conduct in-depth marketing and website analyses.

Interns are also helpful for events. They can assist with things like name tags, logistics, registration management, attendee communications, and feedback surveys.

Use this litmus test to determine if an intern will be a good addition to your team:

- Can the task or project be broken down into clear, manageable steps?

- Is there adequate time for training and supervision?

- Will the project provide meaningful learning opportunities?

- Does the timeline of the project align with typical duration of an internship?

- Is there a low risk if mistakes are (likely) made?

The next step is to create a job posting for the internship. Your company likely already has a template you can use, but just in case, here's an outline to get you started:

- **Job Posting Title**: Marketing Intern

- **Location**: [Office location/Remote]

- **Type**: [Part-time (if less than twenty-five hours per week) or full-time (if more than twenty-five hours per week)]

- **Compensation**: [Pay per hour/Unpaid]

- **Duration**: [Number of semesters or months/Date range]

- **About Us**: [Company name] is a [brief company description]. We are seeking a motivated marketing intern to join our marketing team.

- **Job Description**:

- **Responsibilities**:

- Support social media content creation and scheduling

- Assist with market research and competitor analysis

- Help organize digital marketing assets

- Support email marketing campaigns

- Assist with event planning and execution

- Track basic marketing metrics and create reports

- **Requirements**:

  - Currently pursuing a degree in Marketing, Communications, Public Relations, or a related field

  - Strong written and verbal communication skills

  - Proficiency in Microsoft Office Suite

  - Basic understanding of social media platforms

  - Strong attention to detail

  - Ability to work independently and as part of a team

- **Open to**: [Juniors/Seniors/All eligible applicants]

- **Reporting Structure**: [Who this intern will report to]

- **What We Offer**:
  - Hands-on marketing experience
  - Mentorship from experienced professionals
  - Paid internship (if applicable)
  - Flexible schedule
  - Networking opportunities
  - Potential for future employment
- **How to Apply**: Please send your resume and cover letter to [email] with the subject line "Marketing Intern Application – [Your Name]."

SEARCHING FOR INTERNS

The easiest way to find interns is by contacting the right people at local colleges and universities in your area:

- Career Services Department
- Event coordinators for campus job fairs
- University job board coordinators
- Department heads for marketing, business, communications, and English majors
- Local marketing associations, such as the AMA (they usually have a junior AMA as well)

If you are reaching out to local universities via email, below is a template you can use (email enhanced with AI):

Subject: Marketing Internship Opportunity with [Your Company]

Hello [Name of Career Services Director],

I'm [Your Name], [Title] at [Company], and I'm reaching out to share our job posting for marketing interns from [University Name].

Our marketing team offers hands-on experience in

- Market research
- Budgeting and KPIs
- Social media management
- Content creation

We provide

- [Paid/Unpaid] positions
- Flexible scheduling
- Direct mentorship
- Real project experience

I'd love the opportunity to discuss our internship program and ways we can connect with your students. Could we schedule a brief call next week?

Thank you for your time and consideration!

Best regards,

[Your Signature]

(You can go to https://bit.ly/DiggPlaybook for additional resources, including ready-to-use templates, related to Step 4: Beyond the Org Chart: How to Scale with Internal Allies and External Experts.)

PROVING YOUR WORTH (FROM STEP 5)

In marketing, you will lead many projects, but the completion of those projects on time and under budget is not the most important metric you should be tracking. Instead, you need to align your projects to specific business outcomes and goals.

Below are examples of how to reframe the metrics you report for various projects:

Traditional	Business-focused goal
Implementing a new digital asset management system	30 percent reduction in sales cycles because reps can find materials faster
Rolling out updated sales materials across all regions	$200,000 of annual savings in content production costs
Sales/marketing meeting that delivered key initiatives to impact spec share	Two-basis-point improvement in our specification share
LinkedIn engagement increased by 50 percent	LinkedIn leads are converting 30 percent faster than other sources, reducing our average sales cycle by fifteen days

I also recommend introducing metrics for leading and lagging indicators. Basically, leading indicators are early signals that predict future results, like an increase in website traffic that may lead to more sales later. On the flip side, lagging indicators are measurements of what has already happened, such as last quarter's revenue or completed sales.

Leading indicators help you adjust course before results come in, while lagging indicators confirm whether your strategies actually worked.

Once you know what you are tracking, you need to tell the right story. To do this, outline your metrics into three categories:

- Proof of Progress (Are we doing things right?) – This can include milestone metrics and vanity metrics (engagement, impressions, etc.).

- Proof of Impact: Leading indicators (Are we doing the right things?) – Examples of this can be asset adoption rates by sales team or customer feedback metrics.

- Proof of Value: Lagging indicators (Are we driving business results?) – This includes sales metrics and revenue goals.

FAIL FAST, IMPROVE FASTER (FROM STEP 6)

Progress itself creates value.

The 40/80 rule asserts that a 40 percent solution delivered promptly is more valuable than a perfect solution that arrives too late. This "just ship it" principle encourages releasing work at the 40 percent completion mark to gather initial feedback, then iterating to reach 80 percent through structured revisions. Only pursue the final 20 percent toward perfection if the return on investment clearly justifies the additional effort.

By implementing this approach, teams can prevent costly delays, make real-time adjustments based on actual user responses, and significantly improve overall efficiency. This methodology embraces the value of imperfection as a pathway to better, more market-aligned final products.

FINAL THOUGHTS AND CHAPTER HIGHLIGHTS

Throughout this book, we've explored the practical tools and frameworks that make scaling your team and earning a seat at the executive table possible. Let's take one final look inside this toolbox you've built:

Prerequisite: How Do You Eat an Elephant? You will always have more work and more projects than you have capacity. Remember, it is impossible for all the projects on your list to be a top priority. Therefore, you must narrow down your to-do list to what is truly important. Implement the frameworks we discussed and make sure you don't have more than five "top projects" you are working on at any given time.

Step 1: Fix the Leaks First – Before you start hiring or implementing new technology, ensure you have a well-defined process and that there are no leaks in your bucket. Many times, you will find that you gain extra capacity by simply improving your processes.

Step 2: Technology and AI Tools that Actually Help – Implement and use tools that can help reduce busywork, free up strategic thinking, automate workflows, and eliminate manual tasks. Leveraging technology and AI tools can improve the scalability of your team's efforts by saving you numerous man-hours per month and improving your overall quality of work.

Step 3: Designing a Scalable Dream Team: The In-House vs. Outsource Formula – This chapter introduced a practical scoring framework to help you decide which roles to keep in-house, which to outsource, and how to scale your team efficiently. By focusing on strategic importance, frequency of need, internal expertise, and cost efficiency, you can structure your team to be both agile and cost-effective.

Step 4: Beyond the Org Chart: How to Scale with Internal Allies and External Experts – The traditional, yet still effective, way to scale is by leveraging a variety of in-house and outsourced resources. This includes leveraging team members who are not in the marketing department, hiring interns and freelancers, and outsourcing agencies.

Step 5: Proving Your Worth – In order to get a seat at the table, you need to focus on delivering the work that helps push the business forward. In this chapter, we talked about narrowing down the metrics you track and focusing on three to five key business-driven metrics that you can tie directly to your marketing efforts. We also introduced leading and lagging indicator metrics as a way to more effectively communicate marketing's efforts.

Step 6: Fail Fast, Improve Faster – Setbacks will happen, but the fear of failing will only hold you back. Instead of fearing failure, you should treat it as part of the growth journey, learning quickly and adapting with grace. This will require a mindset shift. With tools like the 40/80 rule and the first-draft mentality, you can move faster, gather better feedback, and build a team that's resilient, flexible, and ready to scale.

Step 7: The Right People, The Right Seats – If you do not have the right people in the right seats, all your other efforts will go to waste. Take a critical look at your team and ensure that you have the right people who will scale with you and, ultimately, help you get a seat at the table.

For additional resources, templates, and worksheets, visit https://bit.ly/DiggPlaybook.

Learn more about how we can work together at www.thediggagency.com.

I look forward to *digging in* with you!

ABOUT THE AUTHOR

Joselyne Walter's journey to marketing leadership was anything but conventional. With a Business Economics degree and aspirations of shaping economic policy in D.C., she instead became captivated by the complexities of manufacturing operations during what was meant to be a temporary college job. That curiosity led her through roles in customer service, supply chain, finance, and logistics, where she managed the dispatch of 36,000 trucks monthly, before finding her home in marketing. Those early experiences shaped her pragmatic approach, blending operational efficiency with strategic marketing execution.

Today, Joselyne leads The Digg Agency, bringing a business-first, results-driven mindset to marketing operations. Her career spans from real estate startups to Fortune 1000 giants and the world's largest manufacturers, where she's built teams from scratch and streamlined processes to drive efficiency. An MBA graduate and certified Toastmaster, she's just as passionate about mentoring talent as she is about optimizing marketing systems. But beyond the boardroom, she finds her greatest joy in life at home with her husband and three young boys, often chasing after them with Lulu, the family dog, in tow. "At the root of it, marketing is about building scalable teams and engines that drive business growth. Sometimes, we just need a practical approach to make it all work."

NEXT STEPS/WORK WITH ME

Connect with me on LinkedIn: https://www.linkedin.com/in/joselyne-walter/.

To learn more about our agency, visit www.TheDiggAgency.com.

If you have questions about working with us, you can reach out via email: information@TheDiggAgency.com.

To download the references and cheat sheets found here, go to https://bit.ly/DiggPlaybook, or scan the QR code below!

www.ingramcontent.com/pod-product-compliance
Lightning Source LLC
Chambersburg PA
CBHW061610120626
46550CB00004B/1675